D1557362

Color Blind

<u>A Mixed Girl's Perspective on Biracial Life</u>

By Tiffany Rae Reid

Founder & CEO
Life Coaching with Tiffany Rae
Building Biracial Relationships and Mentoring

Correspondence should be emailed to
tiffany@tiffanyraecoaching.com or mailed to
P.O. Box 2102
Voorhees, NJ 08043

First and Foremost I want to Thank

My Heavenly Father

and

Personal Savior, Jesus Christ

To

My Mother, My Father, My Sister

And

My Dearest Phil

Without you none of this would be possible

Because of you,

I am on my way to becoming

All that I am supposed to be!

Acknowledgements

This book is dedicated to all of the people in my life who saw me for all that I had to offer this world. Whether you allowed the color of my skin to alter your perception of me or whether you failed to take the color of my skin into consideration when assessing my feelings or opinions, in some way, you were a part of making this book what it has become.

I could not write this book without thanking all of my spiritual teachers: Pastor William Conaway, Bishop David G. Evans and Dr. Stanley El. I especially thank the people who encouraged my writing during many a long-winded conversation: Barbara Reid, David Buckey, Professor Cheryl King, Philip Saunders, and Lenita Galloway-Patton.

To the rest of my family and friends, I thank you for your friendship and for listening to me and conversing with me. I value you more than you will ever know. I look forward to the dialogue continuing for a long time to come.

Cover Work by Dr. Stanley El, D. Div.
CEO/Founder NSABO

"Go now, into the world in peace and know how much an old world needs your youth and gladness~ Recognize that there are words of truth and healing that will never be spoken unless you speak them, and deeds of compassion and courage that will never be done unless you do them~ Never mistake success for victory or failure for defeat~ Know that you were created not for happiness but for joy, and that joy is to them alone who, sometimes with tears in their eyes, commit themselves in love to God and to their brothers and sisters" ~ Amen

Frederick Buechner

Preface

Having finally come to terms with my racial heritage and being comfortable with my chosen racial identity, I understand that a major part of my purpose is to educate, comfort and inspire other biracial people. My life's journey has allowed me to explore my racial and spiritual beginnings and connections and now more than ever, I am very aware of the need that I have to be available for others who are experiencing this same or similar journey. Through this awareness I am dedicated to finding ways and opportunities to share all of the gifts, talents, knowledge and abilities God has given me with others who look, think and feel just like me.

Today my new role allows me to interact with real people. When giving community workshops and presentations I continue to be amazed at the effects that my words and my story have on others. I am proud that I have been able, through the grace of God, to use my biracial experiences in a way that brings clarity, comfort and understanding to biracial individuals.

With each workshop that I present within my community I have interactions with parents raising biracial children that give me pause. Given my mixed racial heritage, many parents approach me after workshops to inform me that they too share and understand the struggle I just described. They in turn tell me details of the many challenges and obstacles they and their families face due to the fact that they are raising or caring for biracial children.

Educators describe the struggles they have in classrooms as they attempt to teach and inform while held in the grip of an educational system that disapproves of celebrating minority characteristics and histories. There has been an undeniable shift from teaching and shaping children towards prepping students for exams. Business owners, admittedly intrigued by someone openly talking about race, cultural diversity and color, seek me out to discuss how they too can create an opportunity for a discussion in their boardrooms that would engage employees and executives alike.

When approached by parents, I am told how proud they are to be raising biracial children without regard to skin color, race or culture. With every admission it becomes harder and harder to hide the shock on my cringing face. Don't get me wrong. I am happy that these parents are seeking help and instruction but I am increasingly overwhelmed at the total disregard that these parents express for their children's welfare and the lack of awareness they seem to have when it comes to their biracial child's overall process of racial identity development.

Caring and loving parents are, in essence, denying the very traits and characteristics that make their biracial children unique and remarkable. This inability to "see" their biracial child's skin color, as it relates to the life experiences and challenges that are innately embedded with that color, is a problem. In my opinion this phenomenon, at its very core, can end up cutting deeper than any knife. In fact, it can strip away more than just a biracial child's inability to understand race as a factor in all levels of physical and psycho-social development.

Not too long ago, I was busy writing and outlining the book of my life. The more time I put into describing personal experiences that happened to me during my childhood, the more time I found myself dwelling on the stories told to me by workshop attendees and the faces of their biracial children. I couldn't escape the emotional pulls that tugged at my heart as my mind revisited images of biracial children being raised in the same conditions and with the same disregard as I experienced growing up in an all white household.

There came a time when it seemed more important to write some sort of guide or instructional manual to the individuals who were raising or impacting the lives of biracial children than for someone to hear the story of my life. Then "it" hit me and I realized that by writing about the story of my biracial life I could in fact help people. By openly talking about the events and experiences that helped to shape the biracial woman I am today, I could prevent someone else from experiencing hurt and pain or at least minimize their exposure to the source.

First and foremost, I want to celebrate parents, caregivers and family members who are raising biracial children. It is important for me that they acknowledge their role and responsibility in their biracial child's life. By allowing themselves to be led by their hearts and opening their lives and their worlds to a child of color they are ultimately opening themselves and the world up to a greater love. It is only through love that we can conquer all negativity, chaos, confusion and hate.

Secondly, I feel a need to comfort and protect biracial children from the colorblind ideology and mentality that had an everlasting impact on my life. I want mixed race children to know that they too can connect with their roots no matter their age or the environment in which they may currently live. In the same way I was led to construct a productive racial identity during my late twenties and early thirties, mixed race children have options and resources that they can tap into when trying to feel out what is right for them.

Third, it is clear to me that with the introduction of *Color Blind* to mainstream media, educators, communities and families, the biracial community has a voice that gives breath to a dialogue and conversation about something much greater than race. Together, by acknowledging the crises and chaos that the expression of colorblindness can create in a biracial child's life, mind and heart, I hope to eradicate colorblindness from every family, school, neighborhood and policy maker's boardroom. In this way, I believe that the racial and cultural heritage of biracial, mixed race, multiethnic, and multiracial children can be identified, discussed and celebrated with "freedom, liberty and justice for all!"

Table of Contents

Color Blind

A Mixed Girl's Perspective on Biracial Life

Table of Contents

Color Blind

A Mixed Girl's Perspective on Biracial Life

APPENDIX

NOTES

REFERENCES

Prologue

We have all seen it somewhere. A cozy town located directly in the middle between here and there. Colorful neighborhoods separated only by giant, mature trees and perfectly manicured landscapes and lawns. Flowering plants and beautiful trellises line the windows and doorways of each and every home.

Average families take time to preserve their belongings in order to maintain an average lifestyle. While most of these homes are average in their appearance from the outside, once penetrated, each threshold gives way to quaint living spaces. In time these reverential places reveal items and possessions that are unique and specific to the individual hearts that reside within.

Sometimes, the only discerning items that can distinguish one family from another are found deep within a home, away from prying eyes and hearts that are full of judgment or scorn. Tucked away in family dens or formal dining rooms are family photos and candid pictures of moments and events that tell the tales of love, surrender, happiness, conquest and sometimes even death. Within these photos, if one looks closely enough, one can determine the feeling and sense of times gone by.

The context of a photograph can paint the true picture of what the person was feeling and doing when posing for the shot. Whether taken for the unexpectedness of the moment or to capture a moment in time forever, it is the collection of these unguarded moments that, when inspected years or generations later, tell a much greater story about the people and places depicted and frozen forever in time. A family's history can be traced by following the clues left in their photographic collection.

If you look even closer, you can pick up a hint of regret. Even closer and you may find a longing for someone or something. In fact, when the context of a photograph is truly considered, a family photo can reveal the true inner workings of the collective mind or emotion.

The photo can reveal what a person valued most in life. It can stand as a loud testament to the quiet beliefs and opinions the person or family held about things such as religion, race, politics and life. If your family is anything like the members of my family, then your bookshelves and treasure chests contain album after album of photos that capture the myriad of moments that make up the meaning of your life.

Your family photos tell a history and stand as one of the most endearing methods used to capture your legacy's unique tale. Page after page after yellowing page, your family photo album captures the players in your family's game of life. Album after album after dust-covered album the pages contain a kind of road map, a historical document if you will, that pinpoints the places where moments and feelings were shared. They find a way to summarize the true essence of who we were and who we have become.

Our photographs showcase the very best and the very worst of what we have to offer. Whether it is our goodness or potential, in a blinding flash, our make or break moment is captured and forever preserved in the home or heart of someone we will look back on one day and say that we loved. It will be seen by many and showcased in its rightful place; as a piece to be remembered in the center of our lives.

Looking back at my family photographs I remember the effort it took to hide my confusion when I would see a photograph appear that did not resemble the image I had of myself. I remember the excitement my family shared as we gathered to commemorate an event or a specific moment in time.

From the time the photo was taken to the time the Polaroid was produced my excitement would turn to dread as the focus of the moment turned from the fantasy of the photo to the reality of my biracial existence.

While my family's photos were mostly random and candid, shouts of, "Tiff, fix your hair!" were heard every time. Our faces and poses reflected the feelings we had toward the picture taker (our beloved mother) who always appeared frantic in her attempts to capture our fleeting moments. Frantic to build a photo album of proof for the inner workings of her color blind mind.

Going through all of my photographs now, I remember almost every detail of each moment captured throughout my life. Most memorable are the photos taken of me and my sister during Easter- my favorite holiday. I especially recall the moans of my sister as she did all that she could to avoid the lens of my mother's camera from finding her or focusing on any one part or feature of her body or face.

And then there was the moment when I could finally put on my Easter dress that I had waited months to actually bring home after spending hours at the local Hills store trying on dresses and accessories. After being forced to give up possession of my favorite dress to the girl working in the lay-a-way department it seemed like years before my mother and I would return to the store to pick up the paid off package that contained all of our holiday gear.

Looking back at these photographs now, I see a girl bubbling with excitement and aware that this very moment was being captured on film. I remember my impatience as I would run to my camera wielding mother, reaching for her arms and hands eager to be the first to catch a glimpse of the photograph as it pushed itself out of our seventies model Polaroid. I was addicted to these photographs.

I loved that they captured something that wasn't always felt. I reveled in the happiness of my mother seeing me and my sister together: the smiles and embraces. For me, I loved the chance to be close to my sister, feeling her arms around me and seeing her smiling, even if it was just to capture a moment in time.

I can't speak for my mother and how she felt when our family photographs came out of her Polaroid. I do know that I felt very different and out of place during those moments when my mother would show our family picture to her guests and friends. I was always very aware of the contrast in how I felt when the pictures were being taken versus when the photos were shown or displayed to the rest of the world. I also know that I wasn't the only one contemplating the way the photos made me feel.

I remember many times when our loving mother would show us very brief moments wherein her reality of our family situation didn't match the image she carried in her heart or in her mind. There were moments when I would catch her staring at a photograph just taken. She would glance at me and then at my sister. In her eyes I saw the challenge that presented itself: a challenge that would never be uttered out loud by my mother until more than twenty years later.

It is the collection of these moments that I have come to understand as the brief breakdowns in time in my mother's mind. It was during these moments when my mother viewed our family photos and responded to a need to rationalize her colorblindness. Within these moments, as in every other endeavor in our lives, I believe that my mother found what she needed to have in order to raise me with our all white family and in her all white life.

And with the addition of every new photograph to our family collection, I was constantly reminded about just how physically different I appeared when compared to my mother and my sister. I loved the many occasions when I would walk the "runway" in the hallway of our apartment. Wearing my mom's hot pink high heels and one of her long, straight wigs, I was allowed to act like someone other than who I really was.

In my mind I imagined that I was a fashion model, stopping to pose for photos before being whisked away to make a music video with some rich and famous pop star. Even in this scenario the end result was always the same. After the shoes were put away and the wig was combed out, I was left holding an ugly memento. On display for all to see was a photograph, a very real and constant reminder, of all that I was and all that I was not.

For me, while I felt that my mother's collection of family photographs was a way to document the holidays and special occasions, I also felt that something else entirely was going on. I felt that in some way, she was looking for something; something that resembled an explanation, a reason, or maybe just an easy way out of feeling guilt and shame. To this day, almost thirty years after most of the photographs were taken, I can't tell you what she feels when she looks at these photographs now.

What I can tell you is what I remember. My mother would stare at our family photographs and look away with this gleam in her eye that told me that she saw something very different than what actually existed in the photographs that she took. I only had to go to her, allow her to put her hand on mine or let her run her hand over my hair in order to make her realize that there was something wrong with what she was trying to do.

Today, when I visit the homes of my friends and family, I see family photographs that capture the new modern family; blended with the addition of a child, due to adoption, the acceptance of a spouse's child from a previous relationship or the product of an interracial union. These photos are diverse in their representation of mixed colors and cultures. Smiling faces represent the hearts of men and women who, no matter the reason, have accepted a child of a different culture or race into their family.

Like my own family photo albums, these family photographs tell a very dramatic story of love and acceptance being chosen over fear and prejudice. Eduardo Bonilla-Silva in *Racism Without Racists* puts forth an idea that expresses the following:

> "*Storytelling is central to communication. To a large degree, all communication is about telling stories. We tell stories to our spouses, children, friends, and coworkers. Through stories we present and represent ourselves and others. Stories have been defined as, 'social events that instruct us about social processes, social structures, and social situations.'*" [1]

In my world, my life's story was told to me through the photos that stick to the yellowing pages of my family's photo albums. Depending on who you are, what you do, and how you identify racially, it is my hope that you walk away from my story, just like me: totally and inexorably transformed. I hope that you will read my story and know that it is a story that allows me to redefine for me what it means to be biracial in today's world.

For me, my family's photo album tells a story that originates in confusion and fear. While my story began with lies, which inevitably created a hole, it is sprinkled with forgiveness and points to the thing that really matters in the end: the heart. But the end has not fully come yet.

While I have gained a sense of understanding, my story continues. The story told so far consists of words that convey pictures that capture moments of my biracial life as I learned to come to terms with my mixed racial heritage while a member of a color blind family. The following account describes what it was like to be biracial without an outlet or connection to the person, community or legacy from which my color is derived. It also provides a soul map to the hearts that helped me to become an active participant in a world that, over the years, was not sure how to take me or treat me given that I never fully fit into a box with which others could identify.

PART ONE
Color Blind
A Mixed Girl's Perspective on Biracial Life

One

Color Blind

Growing up, I was surrounded by a sea of white faces that resembled my mother, my sister, their friends, my peers and my ghost father. To me, this crowd was like water and I was the log floating in it, being carried this way and that way. On some days I felt like I was a part of this body of water and on other days I felt like the water was a part of me. No matter how rough the water surface became or how the direction of the currents threatened to pull us apart, we were one in the same and inseparable.

While they were white in all that they did and all that they said, they were all that I had and all that I knew. My sister and I: inseparable. My mother and I: two sides of the same coin. While I didn't know (at that age I could not have comprehended) how we were held together specifically, I knew from a very early age that whatever was holding us together was stronger, greater and more powerful than the things and people that would try to tear us apart.

It didn't take me long to realize that I was blessed to have my mother as my mother. She had a way about her that made people smile and laugh out loud. And yet, given her tendency to interact socially with others the thing I remember most about my mother is how I saw her act and feel when no one was around. When I caught her in her quiet moments, she appeared sad and lonely. While in her reflective moods, she would scoop me up, hold me close and tell me how much she loved me.

I imagine that my mom was like most other moms: running average households, keeping track of their children and doing what had to be done to put food on the table. She did all of this while attempting to capture every moment of my childhood with photographs. With the exception of the noticeably absent father figure in almost all of the photos, our family photo albums are replete with photos of my naked bum in a water pail and my sister and I in beautiful Easter dresses and silk ribbons in our hair.

Our family photo albums contain hundreds of shots of my sister and I. In some we are sleeping, appearing as two princesses napping on the couch or on the floor. My sister's hair would be spread across the pillow as our arms are seen clutching our favorite stuffed animals. In others we are seen reaching towards one another with a quiet knowing and a sense of comfort that years later we would be forced to admit that neither of us ever really found. I always figured that these types of photographs were considered normal in everyone else's household. That is until I saw the first real break in my mother's heart.

When I was around seven or eight I remember a time when my mother had some of her friends over to the house. I remember the group of women talking, their words interrupted only by their ear splitting laughter as they reminisced about this one's ex and their collective escapades that saw them steering 1970 styled sedans on route 90 between Erie, Pennsylvania and Cleveland, Ohio. On this one particular evening I remember my mother calling to me from the kitchen asking that I bring her one of our family photo albums from the dusty shelves of our bookcase in the living room.

I remember feeling right at home as I found a comfortable place in my mother's lap after handing her the picture book of memories you would have to see in order to believe. My mother opened the photo album on my legs and began flipping through the pages looking for the picture that was going to prove some frivolous point to her small group of friends. As my mother was flipping the pages, I remember looking at the faces of the women who were sneaking looks into the very hearts of our seemingly normal lives. To acknowledge the feelings of fear and rage that began to creep up my neck and fill my little body would mean that I would have to acknowledge what I saw on the faces of these women as their gaze traveled from a certain photograph then to my mom and then to me.

With their minds they were thinking the very same thoughts that I had and with their eyes, they were asking the very same questions that I found my heart asking in the middle of the night. These feelings always came to me in the middle of the night when I couldn't escape feeling so very different from my mom and my sister. In fact, these feelings were so strong that they constantly threatened to overtake me and the meaning of any truth that may have, for any moment of time, existed in the words spoken by my loving, caring and very white mother.

It wasn't long before my mother caught onto the judgmental creep that made its way from her pale skin to my tanned complexion. What first began as a tensing of my body she became aware of as she too caught a glimpse of the unspoken that was being exchanged between her best and childhood friends. At that moment and before she found what she was looking for, my mother quickly closed the photo album and suggested I go back to the living room to play.

Not wanting to acknowledge what we had both just experienced, I did as she asked. To this day we have never discussed her failure to dismiss me before I bore witness to the breaking of her overwhelmed heart. That same night, I remember

3

making an unspoken promise to my mother that I would never be like these women she called her friends. To my mother I silently promised never be the reason why she would ever feel that way again.

As much practice as my mother had at acting normal while loving and raising her biracial child, everyone around us didn't perceive the type of color-blind love she expressed towards me as normal. Neighbors, coaches, teachers, pastors, strangers, even my sister- they were all proud of themselves for asking the questions that I wouldn't have the courage to utter to my mother. In fact, I was in my early twenties and still unable to shield myself from the bombardment of questions and comments made by curious onlookers and nosy neighbors.

I still didn't feel that I had a right to ask my mother about the identity of my father. Doing so would have implied that my father was something other than what my mother had already said he was. Not that I didn't want to ask because there always some part of me that felt that it should be ok if I knew who he was and where he was.

The significance of the photographs in my childhood album was just the start of the story of my life. The collection of memorabilia that my mother found a way to preserve without regard to any of my obvious and apparent differences was, in her own way, just something mothers do with and for their daughters. For me, the collection of every piece of my childhood puzzle and the framing of every photograph was a new rock that was used in the building of an unrealistic wall (a barrier for me and a safe place for her) that would keep us from talking real truth about love, life, race and family for many years to come.

In fact, the "many years to come" find me now, in my mid thirties going through my photo albums and wondering how other parents or families are doing it. How are they raising biracial children and balancing the overall quality and feel of familiar family photos with the reality of a very harsh world that seems stuck in its ability to move past race and the color of a person's skin? How do they juggle taking family photographs with the shock of color that pervades the otherwise monochromatic photo that is being sent out as Christmas cards, decorating their table-tops or adorning fireplace mantels? If they are operating within the same precepts, as did my mother, do they not realize that their colorblindness prevents them from seeing what the world actually sees?

Just like my mother, many of us want to believe that we are living in a colorblind society. We want to think that we have gotten past allowing the color of people's skin to cloud our judgment and opinion. We have a desire to believe that our personal lives are no longer blemished or concerned with race. There are some of us that actually wake up in the morning feeling that race no longer matters in our lives, in our thoughts or in the way we perceive others.

I was born to a Hungarian mother and an African American father. In all that I knew, all that I learned, all that I did and all that I said, I lived a very white life. For the majority of my formative years I was isolated from the identity and cultural history of my black ghost father. I now spend moments of every day playing catch up and trying to figure out which parts of my blackness feel good to me.

The important thing is that it is finally about me. Instead of continuing to dedicate large portions of my day or time making others feel comfortable I think I have finally figured it out. I think I know that in order for others to be comfortable around me, I have to be comfortable inside of myself.

5

Two

Name Calling

Blackie, zebra, redbone, high yellow, and colored-just a few of the words I can remember being called by whites and blacks while growing up. There was a part of me that was not bothered when called these names because I was ignorant as to the meaning of such words. What did bother me however was the feeling that I was left with upon seeing the face and the smirk of someone using these words to address my situation or me.

There was a look in their eyes and a feeling in their mouths that would make its way to my soul. I shudder now to recall the *feeling* that came out of these people when they spoke these words. The feeling is what would make me want to cry and run away; the *words* never hurt me.

I grew up without access to the truth about my racial and cultural heritage. I went without an explanation about the difference in my skin color as compared to the skin color of my mother and my sister. I had no understanding of what it meant to look and feel as I did and all of these things, these lacks if you will, made me want to separate from the world that existed as I knew it.

I believe that good intentioned families are unconsciously committing the acts and omissions that I experienced. Parents and caregivers are themselves raising children of color while under the influence of a colorblind mentality. Knowing the depth of feelings, the highs and lows, which I experienced while being raised and loved in an all white household and knowing the issues and challenges that consumed me well into my early adult life, I believe that colorblindness is a phenomena that exists to the detriment of all families.

In my experience, **Colorblindness** is: <u>the act of raising biracial children without regard to the significance of the color of their skin.</u> It is my belief that colorblindness is becoming a dangerous trend in the households of biracial children. The repercussions of failing to acknowledge the race or ethnic background of a biracial child usually results in harm and creates crises in the lives and identities of our biracial children.

Most of the information being written in literature and documented in movies about the lives and experiences of mixed race children, multiracial or blended families and biracial couples tend to focus on the negative. These brief snippets into the lives of this fast growing demographic tend to focus on the issues and obstacles that exist without giving proper consideration to the context of our lives. Long drawn out scenarios receive accolades when they are centered on the adversity of our daily lives. The most memorable stories that grace our television or movie screens remind us of just how ugly our country's history was and can be when it comes to "race mixing."

Consider for example the story of Thomas Jefferson's slave, Sally Hemmings who birthed children with Jefferson but lived a life unknown to mainstream media. While ignored by all political pundits and generations of Jefferson family members until recent DNA testing validated her Presidential lineage, Hemmings' life was portrayed by the media as a love story, as if she had a choice to choose who owned her, loved her and ultimately denied her. There are the exceptions to every rule and yes they even exist in media.

There is a movie entitled, "Mr. and Mrs. Loving" featuring Lela Rochon and Timothy Hutton that documents the true story of an interracial couple whose arrest in 1958 led to the famous Supreme Court miscegenation case. While this movie demonstrates the personal and political struggle of the couple, most films and television shows tend to depict something entirely different than the reality of the racial situation that existed back in the day. Blatantly missing today is the reality that continues to exist for many interracial individuals living and loving in today's world.

Staying true to my life experience, I am familiar with hearing the racial epithets that other kids call biracial children. Some of us, depending on the generation in which we lived and thrived, heard about burning crosses in the yards of biracial couples after they moved into a monoracial neighborhood. To this day I hear horror stories of the pressures felt and comments overheard by multiracial families as they attempt to introduce their family members to the outside world in which they work, play and live. Our news programs can't find balance or ratings without reminding us on a daily basis of what can happen when people of the world do not respect differences that exist in language, religion and culture.

While I personally experienced all of these things (except the burning cross in my front yard) the one thing that continues to haunt me is people's inability to accept the constant transformation and evolution of my biracial identity. While some people I meet remind me of their disdain for "race mixing" there are others that leave me with a similarly uncomfortable feeling as they try to force my appearance, my diction and even my personal behavior into a box that is comfortable for them. It is this extreme, irrational behavior that frightens me the most.

9

Given the very dynamic nature of my relationships with my family and friends, I appreciate people who openly put forth their true feelings and views about their racial philosophies and opinions. At least in this way, I am prepared to interact with them given their true nature and I am in a better position to coordinate my response to and efforts in getting to know the person and their intentions for getting to know me. In the beginning of any situation I like knowing where other people stand and what they feel when they see me, judge me and learn of my biracial identity and cultural influences.

However, when considering the factors that influence how people learn about one another, the issue that concerns me the most deals directly with how people refuse to acknowledge racial and cultural legacies that are associated with the color of a person's skin. It is my experience that the individuals with the most potential to impact the lives of biracial individuals are the very same people who refuse to see or acknowledge the color of people's skin. In this way, these colorblind individuals, many of whom can be found educating, raising or working with biracial people, pose the loftiest threat to the development of a positive and healthy racial identity for mixed race individuals.

For all of the people suffering from colorblindness, please allow my story to be more of a guide rather than a cautionary tale. Due to the lack of long standing research and information regarding the realities of biracial children, I feel a need to document my own life experiences for those not familiar with our unique life perspective. It is my hope that this book will help biracial children as they endure situations and experiences that will ultimately help them form their racial identity.

It is my hope that this book offers some sort of comfort, assistance and knowledge to those individuals involved with raising or impacting the lives of biracial children. By making a commitment to understanding the very unique experiences had by all mixed race individuals, a dialogue can be initiated and developed that will engage and empower families, peer groups and educators. From this dialogue I hope that all people will begin to understand the layers of freedom that come with acknowledging color as it relates to the history, legacy, experiences, prejudice, opportunities and identity of your biracial child.

By acknowledging what being "of color" really means in our society today, you are opening yourself up to unique and rare opportunities to help celebrate the diversity that forges new relationships. By deepening the understanding of interracial interactions, we can increase the levels of love and acceptance in our personal relationships and within our world at large.

Authors of *Raising Biracial Children*, Kerry Ann Rockquemore and Tracey Laszloffy state,

> *"The 'invisibility of whiteness' can easily lead white parents to assume that racial issues do not concern them. They may believe that the impact of race is an individual choice, and if they only choose to avoid talking about race and not make 'an issue of it,' then no race-related challenges will arise."* [2]

It is with this very same nature and with this very same mentality that my Hungarian mother raised her two daughters. One daughter appeared white (born to an Irish father), had brownish blond hair and resembled the best traits offered by her mother

11

and father. I was the "other" daughter. Biracial in all of my glory, I was always tall for my age. I had kinky hair that no one knew what to do with. To top it all off I had hazel-green eyes and European facial features.

In all of my early childhood photos I appear tan at best. Maybe this is my mother talking through me but even now when I look back, it appears to be true. Now a days people wouldn't call me tan. While they may refer to me as many stereotypical things, most people today would and do refer to me as a light-skinned black girl.

Growing up there was no acknowledgment from my mother or my family that I was black. Although there were suggestive questions and empty stares there was never a reason to refer to myself as anything other than white. But if anyone passing by or catching a glimpse of my tanned skin or green eyes became confused about my racial make up or heritage, you can be sure that my head full of curly locks gave it all away.

Three

Whether in photographs or in person, while others saw a child of color, my mother saw no color at all. I remember several times when my mother would tell others about the frustration she experienced, having divorced her husband (my sister's father) and left alone to her own devices. With her arm around my white sister, my mother would tell people that she was responsible for raising two wonderfully, bright, girls.

Being so young and hearing this, I was absolutely convinced that the only word my mother omitted was white. Looking at the two of them standing their, no one was the wiser that what my mother really meant was that she was left alone with a white daughter to raise a biracial daughter on her own. As a bystander, watching this familiar scene unfold from afar, I would see the gaze of common understanding pass from the other person to my mother.

I would hear offers of help and assistance be extended to my mother as her situation struck a chord with her pious audience. I was also keenly aware of how these offers never came when I was in the picture. I became all too familiar with the gaze that would fall on me, then move toward my scalp and jump to my mother's white skin. It seemed to me that the interpretation of my mother's situation changed drastically when her audience failed to be able to relate to the shocking reality of her plight.

Some of you may consider these examples as too extreme as I attempt to demonstrate the degree of colorblindness from which my mother suffered. Before you make excuses for her unconscious behavior,

13

let's determine what it is that we are really talking about. The term "color blind" is defined as:

1. Existing in an unfortunate state wherein a person is partially or totally unable to distinguish certain colors
2. Not subject to racial prejudices and
3. Not recognizing racial or class distinctions.

Each of these definitions means something different to me and to my personal situation depending on the time frame in which certain life experiences occurred. Each of these definitions also means something different depending on whether you are white, black or biracial. If you are white and you claim to be color blind than I immediately picture you living a life spent around people of color. Maybe you lived in a colorful neighborhood, fell in love with a person of color or maybe you attended a church that had an integrated congregation.

With this picture in my mind I am convinced that your inability to *see* color deals equally with the number of interactions you have had with people of color and with you having rarely ever *felt* someone discriminate against you for something that you could not change. You may stand against racism and the outward expression of prejudice but you find it hard to believe that the color of a person's skin is in any way significant to the daily life experience that is expressed or mentioned by your friends who are of color. You may find it hard to rationalize how someone of color may feel slighted by a member of another group or class based solely on his or her perception or interaction when that larger group has no minority members.

If you are black and claim to be color blind I think of you to be someone who believes that someone else's opinion on race has nothing to do with you. In some way, if you are black and believe that a color blind ideology has its place in your life then it is my opinion that you are seeking a new way to redefine class, power and privilege. You are attempting to re-write history and the way the effects of slavery and the legacy of the one-drop rule can continue to pervade your world and your place in it.

You have a desire to be judged, not by the color of your skin but by the conviction of your words and the relationships in which you are engaged. Gone from your consciousness are all of the ideas, opinions or thoughts, whether owned by someone else who "lives" in a racial majority or your own, that have set the tone for and in some way, if not every way, defined the very quality, length, limitations and expectations of your life.

If you are biracial like me, then I believe that you are caught somewhere in the middle of these two pictures. In fact I think it is more appropriate to say that we live outside of these two images. Other people call this state of being "living in the margins". I believe that being biracial and claiming to be color blind during some point within our lives, we are really asking and begging to be accepted while being seen for what we really are: different, unique and separated from the majority.

As a biracial individual I have, at one time or another fully embraced all three perspectives. I do not believe that the foundation that allows you to buy into this claim will last past the point when your racial identity is, for the first time, challenged by either a thing or an individual that exists in our external world. As opposed to the obvious color-blindness of my mother, I would not say that I was decidedly color blind during the formative years of my early childhood. I would be willing to say that I had not yet experienced any pivotal event that would cause me to become so aware of my color that I would want to escape it all or end it all as I had come to know it.

Depending on other people's experience with race during my childhood, I can say that there were good days (actual days of bliss) and that these good days outnumbered the days of awareness where I was forced by others to be very aware of the color of my skin. Many days of my early childhood passed and I felt loved, wanted and happy. My family consisted of my white mother, my white sister and me.

We loved one another and it showed. My entire family was white and if white was right then I was cream. I felt like that colored crayon in a box of Crayolas that was put in the same row of white co-lored hues; the colored crayon that was put in the corner to reflect its relationship with the white colors but which also reflected a tendency to be associated with the next row.

While my sister and I were close, I am sure that the seven year age difference between us was reason enough for some of the things that naturally existed to prevent us from being even closer. Even with this being the case, my family and I were able to demon-strate the love we felt for one another openly. We kissed, hugged and embraced and expressed our love verbally without restraint.

Given that I was born in 1975, like every other average family, we didn't have much but we had enough of all of the things that we needed in order to get by. Being "offhue" from the rest of my family nev-er made me doubt whether my mother would be there for me if I fell and scraped my knee. My mother was my world. She just happened to be white.

If I fell asleep watching television, I would wake up and be in my mother's arms. If I wanted candy she would dig through the bottom of her purse and give me all of the change that she would find so that I could go splurge at the local Convenience store. My mother was very affectionate and I remember cherishing the feeling of her hands, as they massaged my scalp and neck.

There was nothing horrible and awful between us. White or not, she would protect me against what she knew to be bad. She would take me shopping when she could afford to and even read to me at night.

We were a family. My sister and I together shared bath water, toys and moments. Making do with what we had, we learned to live within the confines of my mother's color blind world even as my mom and sister tried to "do" my hair.

None of us had any idea of the issues or problems that could arise from undertaking such an endeavor but they tried. It didn't matter that I would leave the house with an Afro decorated with barrettes stuck to the sides of my head. It didn't matter that the kids bullied me and made fun of what I wore, how I spoke and how I walked.

It didn't matter that my hair didn't look like every other black kid's on the block. In my family, within the walls of our home, the time my mother and sister spent with me, loving me, teaching me and being with me, made me feel loved and warm and comforted. These were the good days that I remember fondly and there were many.

Four

Dirty and Different: The Words Children Speak

The bad days inserted themselves into my life as I began to spend more and more time outside of the house. I found myself around people who had very particular ideas about the way certain things should or should not be. These days provided an opportunity for me to become more aware of the behaviors, beliefs and actions of others and it allowed others to become more aware of how very different I looked when compared to my mother and my sister.

Being outside gave me such a sense of freedom that, once I tasted it, I begged my mother to let me out. Being outside allowed me an opportunity to test the skills of my body and fill in the blanks of my mind. From the time that I first found strength and speed in my legs, I began to run.

Knowing my mother was always watching me I was happy to run in circles all around our neighborhood. I would run around our apartment building and have her time me. I would even place items in my path so she could see me hurdle over boxes, bikes and picnic tables. I loved showing off for my mother.

Running within the agreed upon boundaries, I discovered a freedom in feeling the wind against my skin and a confidence knowing that none of the neighborhood kids could catch me. The space around our apartment building was becoming too small for my growing frame and my mother's fear become a reality. I began sneaking over the wire fence that surrounded our housing complex from the thick set of woods that grew less than ten feet from our back doorstep.

19

As my legs grew in length, I began to test the wire boundaries of the fence and the emotional security of my mother. This was one of the few personal acts of resistance I would ever display. I was focused on getting into the very heart of the woods that surrounded our apartment community: the very same woods that beckoned me to come outside and get lost.

With the freedom of being outside I was also free to hear the opinions of all the other kids when it came to me being mixed. With every question that they asked I learned new words. Thoughts and images infiltrated my mind that made me yearn for total isolation.

I felt a need to find the center of the woods and felt sure that I would find some sort of magical ability to hide. Not wanting to be seen or found, the woods eventually became my own personal hideaway. I was the star of my imaginary movie set. Within the depths of these woods I felt free to become any character that I wanted to be. My voice felt free to express any opinion or thought that I felt too ashamed to say in front of someone else.

I remember hundreds of days when I explored these woods envisioning myself on the trail of something big and protected by an unseen, natural force. I would find and follow trails that led to new ravines and hills that were unexplored by young, unimaginative wanderers past. There were days that I swung from vines as I acted out my earliest memories of cartoon heroines. Convinced that I was the last person alive on earth, I spent afternoons finding ways to survive with just the wild animals to keep me company.

I grew taller as I grew older and I had access to more children that wanted to accompany me on my voyages and explorations of my woods. These children consisted more of boys than girls because the girls wanted to stay inside and play with Barbie dolls and baby dolls and didn't want to get dirty. So I played with the boys.

I learned how to talk like they talked and I learned to play as hard as they played. Many times our exploits brought us to the community basketball court where I was forced into learning how to play. I'm sure it was due more to my height than to my skill ability but I ended up becoming so good at playing basketball that even the older boys wanted me to play on their team.

I remember my mother telling me that it was only because I was taller than most of the older boys (standing between 5'6'- 5'7" at the age of ten) that they wanted me to play with them. She told me that they needed the height and wanted to be able to tell their friends that their opponents got beat by a girl. The reason did not matter to me. I was just glad to be wanted and it felt good to be really good at something.

For me life was good. I knew where my home was. I knew who my mother was and I knew that if I went home at the same time every night, which was usually before the street lights came on, a delicious meal would be waiting.

To the kids playing basketball with me, it didn't seem to matter that the lady standing at her front door calling out my name was white. I know it must have been confusing but none of these kids ever mentioned it or made a comment about what they or their parents were really thinking. Anytime my mom made a visit to the basketball court it was always a little awkward even though none of the questions or comments that were verbally expressed were ever made directly to me.

Eventually I became very comfortable playing with this same set of older, basketball playing boys. Not a day went by without one of the boys coming to my house to ask me if I wanted to play on one of their teams. The camaraderie I felt with them on the court finally convinced me to give up the solitude of my private woods once and for all.

I willingly exchanged calloused, dirt stained hands for sweaty socks and hand me down sneakers. Sometimes I wonder if this exchange was the beginning or end of Tiffany in her truest understanding of what it was like to be different and of what it was to be biracial. Everything about my essence changed when I gave up Mother Nature for the sake of popularity in my neighborhood

Days on the court were noisy and full of new experiences all the time. There was always some new character that would show up with a need to prove themselves on the court or in our neighborhood. I remember playing ball, being really sore and sweaty and listening to the guys talk a lot of junk.

There were never really any problems. Most of the discussions came from trying to decide whose turn it was to jump the fence in order to fetch a wayward ball. Sometimes the guys would call each other names and sometimes they would end up in a play sort of fight.

On one particular day, I remember some kid who wasn't even from our neighborhood. He stood out because no one had ever seen him before and some of the guys I was playing with were making comments to him and about him while we played. During the middle of one of our toughest games, I remember this strange kid yelling out a word without raising his voice or moving from his seat on the swing. I hadn't really heard what he said but I guess, looking back at the situation now, I didn't have to hear it in order to feel it. Everything about that day, that moment and my life changed.

The ball dropped and stopped. The players stopped playing and the ball stopped bouncing. Even the pretty girls who would hang out of their apartment windows yelling down to the boy on whom they had a crush stopped yelling. And for some reason, all of these players were looking at me.

I remember wishing I could remember the word that the strange kid had called out. I had never paid him any attention especially since he had never played with me and didn't live in our apartment complex. But I could tell from the way everyone was looking at me that they expected me to respond or react in some way. The problem was that I didn't know how I had been "dissed".

Eventually the boy walked away without uttering another word but the damage had been done. And I didn't even know what it all meant. What I did know was that as soon as the unknown kid uttered it, I felt dirty and different. All the other kids on the basketball court that day seemed to have a confidence in what they were and more importantly, in what they were not.

If only my mom knew what she had gotten my sister and I into. So many years and opportunities had passed for my mom to warn us of evils such as these. I was left unprepared to handle all of the hurt and pain that came with the utterances of ignorant little boys.

Even after running straight home and telling my mom the reason that I was so upset I could not shake the feeling of having been so altered. With less than specifics I was able to recount the day's events to my mother who felt obliged to feed me the same explanation that I was always given whenever anyone called me names. But this time was a little different for both of us.

In my mother's eyes I saw a familiar feeling. It looked similar to the time when she was with her girlfriends in the kitchen and I felt her heart break. I understood that she too had felt the sting of my wounds caused by the venom spoken by this unknown little boy. I figured that asking any more questions or continuing the conversation about my need to know any truth, would only make things worse.

I vowed that very day that I would do the best I could to figure it out all on my own. I didn't know where to start but I knew that if I kept silent and stayed close to my mother then all of the questions would work themselves out. What I didn't know was how I could do this and still avoid all of the kids who were also my friends who now had more questions than I did about who and what I really was.

And just like that, I went from being the tall, basketball playing, girlish, tomboy who always returned home when her white mother called to a colored girl who had just been "outed". Now everyone around me seemed to be confused and very conscious of the fact that I was black. Or was I? They couldn't really tell.

Before this unknown character showed up I spent hundreds of days playing basketball, running around, playing tag and yelling, "You're it!" No one ever outwardly questioned what I was. Then one day this kid shows up and calls me a nigger and no one can think of anything else when they see me.

Five
Secrets and Dreams: Replacing Truth with Fantasy

Very soon after this experience, I remember books becoming my best friend. My appetite was voracious and I began to read everything that I could get my hands on. I would escape from the reality that was waiting for me every time I opened my front door by losing myself in a book. I began to read books about people from other countries and their experiences inside and outside of the world that I knew. I began to read about people who looked very different from me. I had a hard time understanding why the book titles read black instead of white.

My awareness of being different continued to increase exponentially. I began to feel like everyone was keeping secrets from me: my mother, my family, even people at my church. I didn't know why they just wouldn't tell me what was really going on. The feeling only got worse when other people of color came around.With every skin tone of color that I saw, I would start to imagine that maybe, just maybe, white and black meant something more than what I saw in my box of crayola crayons. I felt my tummy tumble when people of color made comments about the color of my eyes being so green or the texture of my hair being so good. I never knew what they meant.

Comments like, "She's a redbone alright" would really scare me. My desire to become a doctor was initiated right there on the spot the first time I heard someone say this to me. I was determined to see inside of a human being in order to see whether it was possible for our bones to actually be red.

So it's obvious that even at that early age, I always knew that I was different in some way from my sister and my mother. As different types of experiences began to add up though I began to notice many more of the similarities between people whose skin was colored white as compared to those whose skin was colored black. In my apartment community, a neighborhood in and of itself, whites and blacks would get drunk and yell a lot; sometimes together or at each other.

I would hear white parents and black parents swear at one another and I noticed that if you took away skin color, all of these individuals pretty much acted and sounded the same. They smoked, they danced, and they took their kids roller-skating. I even met some white people and some black people (but not many black people) who seemed to feel the same way I did about The New Kids on the Block and Miami Vice (well, really just Don Johnson).

Although at the age of ten or eleven I never thought in terms of race, the similarities between whites and blacks kept me questioning my racial identity, especially when my whiteness was challenged. I didn't start focusing on the many and sometimes obvious differences until more kids started showing up and would remind me of just how different I really was.

"Are you adopted?" "Is your daddy black?" Good questions! I just didn't have any answers. And this is the root of many of the problems that biracial children can develop when being raised and nurtured by loving and color blind parents.

While I began to notice and stress out about all of the differences that existed between me and my mother and sister, they all seemed to go unnoticed by my mother. So, like most children tend to do, I started to replace the truth with fantasy and began to daydream big time. When I found myself at church surrounded by a wonderful congregation that allowed my mother the leeway to live in her altered reality, I enjoyed times of peace. This sense of peace lasted only until a black evangelist would be invited to our church to preach the gospel or sing. Then it seemed like all eyes were on the little token black girl sitting in the pew next to the heavyset white woman.

While their gazes told me that they were trying to figure us out, I responded with empty eyes, allowing my mind to iron out the details of the daydream that went a little something like this: curly haired mixed girl separated from black birth mother ten years ago, found when birth mother joined church ministry and returned to town ten years later only to find her long lost child sitting in a pew of the very church the mother had attended before her baby was stolen. Curly haired mixed girl reunited with singer/songwriter mother and come to find out, the young girl can sing too! Then the song would end or we would stand for the customary prayer at the conclusion of the service and I would be reminded of my existence parallel to that of my mother's reality. Here I was: back to the gazes and the looks on the traveling minister's faces that said, "Poor little girl. Her mother doesn't even know how to do her hair."

Yes there was always that. There was always the image of me standing with my mother in front of our bathroom mirror trying to determine what to do with my tight mass of curls. While I was quietly screaming on the inside and sometimes crying on the outside, she would hold me by the shoulders as she used a pik to make my hair really big.

Then, to add insult to injury, she would force barrettes onto the sides of my head and send me out to the hungry wolves in the very confused world in which I lived. Now, I believe that my mother thought that she could use a pik on my hair because her best friend was married to a Puerto Rican man whose best friend was mixed and he walked around piking out his hair. I know that somewhere in my mother's altered reality, she probably liked the image of this guy picking away at his Puerto Rican hair and thought, "hey, that's what I can do with Tiff's hair!"

Well if I didn't even know what I should have been doing to my hair, how could I possibly hold that one against my mom? To this day, my hair is my Achilles heel. It's one thing that reminds me of my biracial struggle, of the days when I truly believed that I was white, and it reminds me of my biracial struggle even now that I know I have some black in me too!

The type of daydreaming that I used to escape uncomfortable situations didn't stop at church. I remember riding in the car with my mom, when front seats weren't separated and you had to move the whole front seat forward if you wanted to get in or out of the back seat. We would be riding in the car and before she knew what was happening, I would scoot over and change my mother's radio station, rolling the ball dial all the way over to the left and slowly back toward the right.

I would never get too far before she would slap my hand away and move the dial back to her pre-selected station. It didn't matter though. Before she had a chance to change the station back, even if only five words of an R&B song were uttered, my mind would be off and racing to a faraway place where everyone looked like me, welcomed me and wanted me.

I would picture the appearance of a black superstar after hearing it announced that he was coming into town for a concert. I saw him ride up in his limousine and claim me as his own. He would take me shopping and get my hair done. We would make the concert venue just in enough time for him to bring me up on stage after the curtain was raised to announce to the whole world that he had found his long lost daughter and wanted everyone to take a good look at his good little girl. Critics and fans alike would express their joy and happiness at their favorite singer of all time finding his long lost daughter. They would turn to each other in their rows of seats and remark, "and she can sing too!"

From a very early age I have been unable to address my mother about the identity of my father. I never knew that I had a right to ask my mother about my father, his color or rather, about my color. For this reason, I believe I began to hang out with my best friend who was Puerto Rican. We immediately established a comfort level that soothed a part of me that craved to know the reason for many of my differences.

I learned to speak Spanish fluently at a very young age and loved being able to speak Spanish with my best friend in the presence of both white and black people, especially my mother. In these situations, I would come to understand years later that what I loved about those moments was the utter lack of attention that I received from a community that accepted me for me and appreciated the effort I took to learn about them, their culture and their language. Hanging out with my Puerto Rican friend's family I no longer experienced the forlorn stares and the "I feel sorry for you" gazes.

No one looked to me and then to my mother or to my friend with curious eyes and disgusting faces. I would let them assume that, just like my friend, I was some sort or degree of Spanish descent. Of course, the situation always came to an end but in my head, with the force field of an imagination that I had built, the scenarios never stopped. Even in my adult life, while working in New York City, if someone mistook me for a person of Hispanic or Latino descent, I never questioned or challenged their misconception or belief.

My mental escapes began to alter my own precious reality. I assume that this happened in just the same way as my mother's reality had been altered over a longer period of time. I was somebody else so often in my own mind that I would sometimes secretly wish that my mother wouldn't show up after school to pick me up or wouldn't clap for me at school performances. At least this way, I could avoid the stares that she seemed too willing herself to ignore or endure.

Just because my mother was able to avoid confrontation with nosy neighbors or intrusive family members didn't mean I was so lucky or able to do the same. With each birthday I was often confronted by groups of increasingly aggressive adolescents. These kids continued to demand, sometimes in earshot of their parent's prodding, to know who and what I thought I was.

They would catch me alone on the playground or walking in the woods and surround me, requiring me to provide an explanation as to why my mother was white. In my head I would hear my mother telling me to run away but something in my heart would not let me. Without a second thought I was pushing back and picking up rocks and sticks, readying myself for a final defense.

To understand the repercussions of being mixed and raised in a color blind household it is important that we discuss what it means to be color blind. For the first eight to ten years of my life I admit that I was just like my mother: I didn't *see* color in the same way as others saw the color of my skin. I didn't *feel* color and I knew nothing about the history or legacy of slavery, discrimination, stereotypes or prejudice. Yeah I noticed people looking at me funny but my mother always told me something funny about the people who we caught staring so they seemed to be the one suffering from something. It was never me.

My mom's inability to see color made me believe that no one else saw color either. I don't believe that her inability or lack of desire to say the word black came from a desire to hurt me or prevent my racial identity from developing. I doubt she thought in terms such as these. But my mother's inability to have a conversation with me early on in my life about who and what I was or how I would be classified by society, prevented me from developing an awareness of how I would be treated, accepted and understood by a world that was just beginning to understand that "race mixing" was not going to make the world stop.

While my mother demonstrated an inability to deal effectively or productively with certain aspects of raising a biracial child, I understand that the experience of other parents, caregivers or family members raising biracial children will not always mimic that of my mother or my own. However, I do believe that there are some aspects of similar testimony and experiences that will resonate with biracial children, their families and peers. It is for these individuals that I write this book.

For instance, not only was my mother color blind but she also flat out lied to me the very first time I dared to ask her about the differences in our skin color. "Mommy, am I white?" You would think this question would trigger an enormous emotional upheaval for my very conservative mother. That probably would have been the best thing that could have happened but it didn't happen that way. As you can guess, my mother resorted to what she knew and did best.

My mother pulled down the well-maintained photo albums from the bookcase and I was shown photos of my Hungarian uncle. He was dark like me. He had curly hair like me. His lips were thick and his eyes were the very same hazel-green mixture, just like mine. He was Hungarian and spoke only Hungarian. Well there it was! This was the proof that I needed. I couldn't wait to go out and tell all of the disbelievers just how wrong they were. What I didn't know was that they had more ammunition than I did. And boy did they hit me with every round of it.

There are too many people just like me who have witnessed first hand all of the devastating power that the word nigger has delivered. It is more than a dangerous word. Like any bullet or grenade, it can kill someone. Like a murderous attack, it can creep up on you no matter the strength of your defenses. Like a stealth bomber you don't even feel it coming until it is too late. And in its murderous course, whether directed at me, near me or delivered because of me, it always found a way to kill some part of me.

PART TWO
Color Blind
A Mixed Girl's Perspective on Biracial Life

Six

While I won't make excuses for what my mother's lies had the potential to do, I now know that my mother, like a lot of women raising children without the support of the parent of color, was dealing with issues of anger and abandonment. The responses that my mother provided to me throughout my life and the way she handled my innate desire to know and grow my personal understanding of my racial heritage and awareness is similar to the responses and behaviors that some women demonstrate. Instead of focusing on the needs of the child, women similar in life experience, resource and support as my mother, cannot stop focusing on their own needs and the issues that they cannot begin to deal with while at the same time, remaining responsible for running households, raising other children and tending to other responsibilities.

What I have come to understand while learning about myself, educating my mother and interacting with other biracial individuals and the people that love them, is that there is a need for our families, neighborhoods, communities, educators, and policy makers to understand how the color blind approach to raising and interacting with the biracial community affects the racial development of mixed-race children. If you find yourself raising a biracial child, only you can go over your life in review and decide which of the definitions, previously given, resonate with the pattern of behavior that best describes how you have chosen to raise your children. Only you can truly understand which of the definitions of color blindness provide or reflect a thought, feeling or sentiment that has impacted your interaction with someone in the biracial community.

Have you ever been one of those individuals that have ever told someone that you don't see race or that you don't consider yourself capable of holding any type of racial stereotypes or prejudices? People, we need to get real. Can we agree that the idea of individuals not seeing race is impossible? Do we agree that we have all, at one time or another within our life experience, learned to associate meanings and characteristics with certain physical traits?

Seeing race and seeing color are two very distinct and different ideas. Seeing race and seeing color is not the same thing as treating another person differently or in a discriminatory way. Most of the people with whom I speak and work with have hearts that are in the right place. They have to be in order to prepare for and endure the unique experiences that come along with raising mixed-race children.

My mother was the perfect example. Here she was, one of seven children, the first generation of her family to be born here in the United States, left to her own devices to raise a child of color. We won't even get into the fact that raising a child of color also meant that she had a child outside of her own marriage. In the nineteen seventies, without resources or someone she could confide in or learn from, my mother's heart was in the right place when she chose to raise me thinking that she was in some way capable of protecting me from the pain that she herself was experiencing.

I can only imagine, compared to the actual number of racial epithets that I heard expressed by my direct family members, the number of words, phrases and hell my mother must have taken from her sisters and brothers, and mother and father when raising me with my sister alone. Today, the idea of children being raised by single and/or divorced parents is pretty common. Add to this demographic be-being biracial and in the nineteen seventies, you didn't find that many around. Without support from her family, friends and my father, I am convinced that my mother did the best that she could with the resources that she had. Today, given the global diversity of the world and the fact that the President of the United States is himself a biracial individual, "doing the best you can" raising biracial children is simply not good enough.

Are you in a similar predicament as was my mother? Are you without support and uncomfortable raising a mixed race child? Are you operating from a place of love and acceptance? Then just like my mother and I you can in fact expect to get to a place in your life where you can openly discuss life experiences on a mutually accepting level with your biracial children.

First you must accept that by living a color blind ideology, you are harming your biracial child. Most parents and family members raising children of color are shocked to learn of the extent of damage that can be done while trying to raise their biracial children within a color blind household or environment. "Understanding racism, prejudices and stereotypes can be challenging for white parents of mixed-race children who, until adopting or bearing biracial children, may have been unaware of the existence, extent or frequency of racism in America today."[3]

Today, many of us live in communities filled with culturally diverse individuals. We may be living next to a synagogue or working near a mosque. Steakhouses are competing with Indian restaurants and sushi bars and it seems like every other month, we are hearing about a new Hollywood starlet that is finding a new and faraway place from which to adopt a bouncing baby boy or girl.

In today's melting pot, we are surrounded by people and relationships that provide various opportunities for us to share and learn of one another's differences, cultural mores and traditions. As people living, working and loving within chosen demographics, we have the opportunity and choice to tap into those characteristics and resources that allow us to relate with other like minded individuals who hold true to the same cultural, religious and racial ideologies that we share. In turn, we find ourselves communicating, learning and passing on those very things that our families, friends and social networks, hold dear.

So what are you passing on? As parents, are you mirroring yourself after your own parents who thought of "race mixing" as bad, evil or something "we just don't do"? Have you found the courage to disconnect from limiting beliefs and negative images? Are you free to love unconditionally and without regard to the historical legacy of what it means to be black, white or mixed? Are you prepared to live every day of your life attuned to the struggle, obstacles and challenges that will meet your biracial child at the door of his or her heart and intellect?

Do you have a support group, place or person that you can go to at a moment's notice in order to refuel your spiritual, emotional and psychological gas tank when the world, your mother or your best friend, drain you of all that you thought you had to give?

Are you ready to learn how to comb and maintain your biracial child's hair and skin? "Have you considered that although you have a lot of love to give, there will come a time when you too are seen by your biracial child as 'one of them' and an outsider to the entire and very personal, internal goings on" [4] that your child will endure as they attempt to come to terms with their own racial identity?

Living in today's modern world, we are privileged to have technology that allows us to use our time and talents differently than people who lived even a single generation before us. Sometimes I wonder how different my life experience, or that of my mother, would have been had she been able to get on the Internet and Google, "help with raising a biracial child". How many resources, organizations, associations, magazines or people would she have found to help her on her journey understanding her role and responsibility in raising a child of color?

How different would she be and have been had she had someone of color in her life to go to in order to ask questions about how to do my hair, how to talk about racial differences, and whether or not it would have been important for me to know about my cultural and racial heritage before I turned twenty two years of age? We will never know how any of this would have played out differently and this is by no means, the point of this book. My mother and I to this day are very, very close. We talk every single day and are able to discuss racial issues in both the white and black communities. The point of sharing with you the stories of my biracial life is to relay the fact that unlike my mother and other individuals from her generation, today we are unique in our ability to put all excuses aside and find help and resources that can empower everyone associated with the biracial community.

Without excuse or judgment, we are able to build bridges that close the communication gaps that once existed which separated people by race and geographic location. Today, if we choose to, we can unite racially and intellectually within our families

39

and our neighborhoods in order to communicate and interact in a prescribed manner that embodies a sense of universal love, respect and an overall acceptance of racial differences and cultural norms. "Frequency of contact is important because this creates the opportunity to learn about others, and ultimately to learn about one's self in relation to others. There simply is no substitute for experience."[5]

Seven

What it Means to be Different

Experience is what I lacked. For the majority of my life I was without experience dealing with people of color. I was raised in an all white household surrounded by a white mentality, white issues, white food, white dress and white people. I had no connection to my parent of color or to the community of color that existed in the next door apartment and just down the street from where we lived.

My mother's color blindness did not extend outside of the door from our home. While she was unable to see the color of her daughter's skin, she was very aware of all of the color that surrounded our home. For instance, one day I came home after our black next-door neighbor braided my hair in cornrows. My mother made me take it out because it was too black. In my mother's eyes, I was white and seeing me identifying or displaying any part of the blackness within me, was too uncomfortable for her. It clashed with the identity and the reality that she had created for her and for me.

By gaining a very basic understanding of the unique life experiences shared by many multiethnic and mixed race individuals, we have an opportunity that did not exist in generations past. Through sharing and loving we are able to do what many researches and scholars have failed to do in the very recent past. We can legitimize the human experience of mixed race peoples and ultimately, erase the solid, racial lines that stop us from realizing the similarities of our differences.

We can embrace the very purpose of some of our most modern technological marvels and conveniences. By doing so, we can establish a baseline of knowledge and understanding of one of the most commonly misunderstood and disenfranchising realities of biracial life. No longer will we be seen as not white enough by white people or black enough by black people.

Biracial individuals have a lot in common with individuals who are from different cultures, speak different languages and carry on different traditions. We all share in the fact that at one time or another, we have been systematically taught that being different or unique is something to be covered up or looked down upon. We have seen and felt that there is something about us that we should be ashamed of and ultimately, in some form or fashion, we have come to accept ourselves as something of a lesser value. We associate our place within society as something that can be diminished.

Many of my family members and friends from foreign countries have relayed to me their experiences of feeling like a second-class citizen because their immediate audience detected an accent. How many times have you stopped in mid-sentence to watch an approaching woman of the Muslim faith; not because she is breaking the law, attacking someone or using profanity but simply because she has chosen to cover herself in public as per the tenets of her faith, culture and religion? Albert Memmi said, "There is a strange kind of enigma associated with the problem of racism. No one, or almost no one, wishes to see themselves as racist; still, racism persists, real and tenacious". [6]

We are all guilty of harboring, displaying or verbally expressing some type of stereotypical or prejudicial viewpoint or opinion. Yes all of us! Blacks, whites, Asians, Latinos, mixed race individuals: all of us. The point is that as a society, as

42

families and as individuals, we have the ability to act right now. Right now we can make choices and decisions to empower one another by learning about one another.

You can go to your local library or book retailer and pull up hundreds of thousands of books on European history and the history of African nations and cultures. You can find books that provide analytical perspectives and opinions on the history of slavery and the colonization of the Americas. Many a novel and period piece capture the mindset and daily life of the indentured English servant.

Researchers and scholars have dissected the history and origin of different types of peoples, races and cultures within these two reference points. Literature has been written and documentaries have been created that outline the cultural norms and mores of people originating from these varied parts of the world. In college classrooms and middle school history books you will even find copies of first hand accounts that seemingly map out the African and European diasporas and the eventual societal breakdowns that occurred based on the amounts and limits of resources.

In contrast to the history lessons that pervade our educational system, very few books exist for the sole purpose of documenting or describing the life experience or cultural phenomena of the biracial individual. Whether from a historical or social perspective there is a large part of our history missing from the collections of words, descriptions of events, life experiences and empirical evidence that currently exist. Members of the biracial community are hard pressed to find texts that speak to their perspective.

In fact, when conducting any type of freshman research, one would notice that biracial life is rarely mentioned as the sheer focus of many texts. In most cases biracial life is mentioned as a reaction to an event in our modern day world that surrounds some sort of racial or cultural controversy, hype or hysteria. For example, for me, it was expedient to be mixed during the O.J. Simpson trial because mixed race individuals were sought after by both whites and blacks in order to reinforce some version of their color blind ideology.

I was asked questions like, "do you really think he did it?" and "he's got to be guilty right?" Whites wanted me to prove that the problem with race relations continues to lie with people of color. They wanted me, and other people who looked like me to, in some way, validate their beliefs, opinions and stereotypes about what it meant to be black.

On the other hand, blacks wanted me, and other people who looked like me, to show some sort of allegiance to their cause. They wanted us to prove for them that black people in general could live and thrive in this ever-changing world without needing or wanting something so bad (something white) that we, like O.J., would kill for it. In each of these cases, white and black people alike revealed to me the degree to which their lives are lived in and dominated by color blindness.

I found myself in a post Civil Rights world where white and black members of society wanted to act like issues such as race and color didn't exist. I found myself asked in a round about way, by both whites and blacks, to reinforce racist ideas and preconceived notions of the other and ultimately of each other. No matter how softly one speaks when expressing their true racial views, when it comes down to it, it has been my experience that whites and blacks find themselves expressing racial tolerance based on prejudicial beliefs.

The existence of these internal beliefs are learned from a previous racist generation or picked up in inappropriate places. The color blind ideology that currently pervades our society cannot continue to exist in its current form. Biracial people may in fact appreciate the effort put forth in outward expressions of acceptance and tolerance by our monoracial counterparts. However, it is my belief that mixed race individuals will begin to seek an alternative form of belonging as soon as they experience a hint of racism or a microaggression in response to a chosen racial identity.

In many of my memorable life altering moments, most of the racial tension expressed by my black and white friends was exhibited in half hearted attempts at real dialogue and heart felt expressions of acceptance and understanding. Eduardo Bonilla-Silva got it right when he wrote, "Color-blind racism's race talk avoids racist terminology and preserves its mythological nonracialism through semantic moves such as 'I am not a racist, but,' 'Some of my best friends are...' 'I am not black, but,' 'Yes and no,' or 'Anything but race.'"[7] Each of the white and black individuals who engaged with me in this questionable dialogue would claim to this day to have experienced positive relationships with their white and black counterparts.

In fact, most of these individuals would begin their inquiries into where I stood on O.J.'s guilt or innocence by telling me stories of their involvement with their white and black friends. With one side of their mouth they would have me convinced that maybe, just maybe they could understand my plight. It appeared that they were capable of understanding how I could feel caught in the racial middle of an ever-changing world and philosophy. Then, with the other side of their mouths, they were challenging my blackness and whiteness respectively; forcing me to choose a side and asking me to help them feel comfortable living in their color blind existence.

I wasn't strong enough in my "mixedness" to appreciate the power of what was really being asked of me by my white and black peers during that time in my life but by the time 2008 rolled around, I was on the path to discovering how unique and remarkable it really was to be biracial. All of a sudden, it was cool to be mixed when then senator, Barack Obama was running for the presidency. Out of nowhere mixed people were identified and brought into every political conversation.

Our opinions were gold and our perspectives were pure truth. We were of course, the closest ideas to the impression of the president that most people were ever going to get. People didn't seem to realize that, even as monoracial individuals are as different from one another as is every snowflake, being mixed didn't mean we were all one in the same.

Based on my life experience, I truly believe that unless the lives of white or black people are altered or drastically changed by a remarkable person of mixed race heritage, biracial stories continue to be overlooked when compared to their white and black counterparts. Topics that document biracial identity development, strategies and experiences that speak to the daily challenges of mixed race peoples are lacking. Hollywood and mainstream literature love to tell stories about people that the majority of society can identify with. I don't think they have quite figured out yet what to do with the millions of stories of uniqueness and remarkable encounters that could be told by people who don't fit society's racial norms.

This is not to say that biracial individuals are not trying to get their stories told. I continue to be inspired and encouraged by the number of male and female biracial entrepreneurs who are creating products catering to the biracial community. I just wish that in all times, not just when society feels it is an opportune time, the same attention and resources were given to the biracial community in an attempt to document, correlate, investigate and eventually celebrate the biracial experience in America as has been given to other cultural and racial genres.

Since this is not the case, I believe that our biracial population is at a unique and powerful place in time. The growing and ever exploding diversity of our world provides us with a chance to reprogram and educate ourselves. By tapping into the power of our unique racial expressions we can develop new ways to identify and celebrate the very things that make us appear different from members of our extended families and peers.

By committing to establish a framework of communication and acceptance, biracial individuals can empower our entire biracial community to exist without excuses. We can teach our community how to express their culture and color with pride and flourish within their families, their communities and ultimately the world. While it's important to focus on what we can do right now in order to prepare us for the future, it's also important to address the past and historical legacy of our nation.

Eight

Racial Identity Development: The Role of the Family

So let us consider the most basic and yet most profound processes that affect the way biracial individuals differ from their monoracial white and black counterparts. I will refrain from visiting the contents found within many if not most of the psychology and social work manuals, texts and materials. My focus with *Color Blind-A Mixed Girl's Perspective on Biracial Life* is to provide insight into the mind, choices, options, life experiences and desires of biracial individuals based on my life experience.

There exist a significant amount of factors that we must consider when trying to understand how biracial children are affected by their internal and external worlds. The racial development and identification process that our mixed-race children endure is one that is rarely discussed and even less understood. [8] Given the number of factors, I suggest that we begin by envisioning an onion with many layers.

Given the way an onion's layers are constructed, let us begin to discuss and understand the factors beginning with the one that has the most impact, potential and power to negatively or positively affect biracial children: *The Family*. I think we can all agree that no matter the condition or degree of any child's circumstance, their immediate family would be the innermost and tightly bound layer in our developmental onion example. Family is at the heart of the developmental process for biracial children, as the family constitutes their idea of the world at large.

It is from this interaction among and between family members that biracial children learn the value of their role within communities (families) and the external stage (the world at large). Parents, caregivers and extended family members who find themselves in charge of "raising" biracial children are the first level of defense. Their response to skin color and hair texture is the first way biracial children learn about race, culture, heritage, traditions, patience, acceptance, understanding, tolerance and love.

It does not matter whether children within the same family share similar physical traits and characteristics (such as hair color and texture, eye color, height, and skin color) with siblings and parents. Appearance can take on dramatic meaning as children come to understand the responses by their immediate defensive team in relation to racial and physical characteristics that society will use to categorize each child as "black" or "white". [9] In fact, there are many holidays and birthdays spent with my family where the appearance of whiteness is all that I can recall.

One Christmas Eve stands out as I remember all the white kids in our family having more gifts than I did under the tree. While an outsider could easily accuse me of misinterpreting this event, there is something that cannot be rationalized: the feeling of being different that settled into my soul while the other kids ogled over their gifts. There was something that shouted out at me as never before.

I remember walking into my grandmother's house and smelling the duck cooking and all the distinct aromas of the Hungarian foods being prepared. I remember the greetings in a Hungarian tongue and the hugs exchanged between my mom and her mother, her sisters and brothers. I remember the adults giving us kids the gifts to run and place under the tree.

I was always excited for this gathering because it gave me a chance to experience my mother in all of her glory having dressed herself and her two girls up in their Christmas finery. She was with her mother and her family and it seemed, for her, that this is what she missed so very much. It seemed that maybe, just maybe, her family would be able to ignore the fact that she had had sex with a black man and had had a mixed kid, for even one cold, snowy night in December.

So here I was, the only person of color in a house full of Hungarians. I remember sitting in a chair watching the rest of the family laugh, hug, and play with each other's hair. They were touching one another and smiling. I remember watching feelings of love escape from parent to child as sleepy kids sat in their parent's laps and rested their heads on the shoulders of their mommies and daddies.

I remember how cold I felt sitting alone. I wished my mother or anyone of her sisters or brothers would find me special and worthy enough to come sit next to me and ask me questions about school or life. I wanted one of them to rub my shoulders and play with my hair. But they didn't know how and I knew this too. So I was forced to deliberately seek out this feeling of love any way that I could. (A pattern that I would recreate over and over again even into my adult life).

I remember flitting from one aunt to an uncle to my sister or my niece. I would make up stories hoping they would want to hear more and stay around me, play with me and show me attention. When that didn't work, I would plant myself in the kitchen and watch my mother and grandmother urge one another on to add more spice to this dish or to baste the duck more or to knead the dough thinner. I would arrive at my grandmother's house starving to taste the delicacies that were being prepared in the kitchen and I would leave starving for affection and love from the people I saw exchanging it freely with others and withholding it from me for reasons I didn't quite understand at that time.

Even today as I interact with young, biracial girls and young women, I find that the most common trait between all of us is that we, at one time or another, were all starving. There are cases where young biracial girls are starving for the love and attention of a white mother who has created a cocoon around her life and around her reality. The mother is oftentimes so disconnected that she cannot even identify the behavior of her biracial child as a cry for love, knowledge, acceptance and ultimately freedom.

Like me, these young girls frantically go from one person to another trying to identify some sort of similar trait or feature. They seek out anything that will prove or disprove an idea that we have created about ourselves. And this cycle repeats throughout most of our lives. We even begin to create an idea or perception about our relationship with our parent of color that may or may not have actually existed.

For me, my black father was an unknown and so I spent a lot of time and energy creating him and defining him in my mind. In this way I was able to spend time with him, converse with him and see myself in him. The image that I created of myself that has lasted throughout my lifetime has a lot more to do with this unbelievable relationship I had with my unknown father than it does with the confusing relationship I had with my mother who was always present.

In this same vein, I believe that there are times when white mothers, after becoming disengaged from the parent of color, are no longer able to connect fluidly to their biracial children in the same way that may seem easier or more natural with children that share a similar skin color and other physical traits. The more involved I become with starving, young, bi-racial women the more I realize that white mothers raising biracial children are in need of powerful resources and mentors. White parents raising biracial children need instruction, guidance and acceptance even more than I previously understood.

White parents raising mixed race kids need help bonding with their biracial children. They need to come to terms with the realities of their children's lives. They need to know that their children, on a daily basis, will be bombarded with positive images of whiteness and not so kind images of blackness.

Just like me, these same starving, young girls, whether their mother is present or not, will search for a father figure for most of their lives that suits their preconceived notions of their parent of color. This reality eventually became the pattern in my life with male teachers, boyfriends, male colleagues and peers, even pastors. At one time in my life, I was so starved for attention and instruction from a male figure in my life that my attempts to rationalize the color aspect even began to diminish.

When confronted with a white pastor in our church or a white youth group leader, I began to picture these men as possible father candidates. I convinced myself that maybe my mother was right and knew what she was talking about this whole time. Maybe I was just a dark-skinned Hungarian and maybe we are attending this church because this is my real father and for some reason he just didn't want to tell me until he felt I could handle it. After all, the pastor had a whole other family to con-sider and I was conceived in love and God would tell all of us when the right time was to bring us all to-gether.

In this way, I found myself beginning to believe in most of the lies and confusing things my mother would say. Under this same spell, I find these young girls today searching for a male figure that is willing to step in to love, teach, and protect them. The problem is that there are too many willing boys and men who are smart enough to recognize the look of starvation in these young girls.

Without much convincing, these manipulative males are promising all that these girls want to hear. Given the level of emotional confusion they are already experiencing in their color blind households, these young, biracial girls are searching for love and acceptance from any source. They present their emotional needs on their sleeves and appear as eager, naïve opportunities for men of ill repute.

As we continue to explore the role and importance of family in the lives of biracial children as they develop their racial identity, it is important to understand that each set of parents: single parents, married couples, parents of color or extended families, are in the position of raising biracial children and don't have many resources to help in this experience. Based on the history of race relations within the United States, there exists a certain societal legacy when it comes to categorizing people of color and their life experiences. "While the relationship between physical traits and racial identity may seem to be straightforward and direct, the reality is more complicated. In other words, a child's physical characteristics do not directly and exclusively determine their racial identity so that those who look black identify as black, those who look white identify as white, and those who look somewhere in the middle identify as biracial."[10]

I don't know how others saw or experienced me when I was younger but I can tell you that thanks to my mother's own issues, I thought I looked white on the outside and I thought that other people saw me as white as well. Black people constantly intrigued me when I saw them. I was taken in with the way they looked at me.

It seemed to me that they recognized me and this was very, very comforting to my soul given that my daily existence with my white family members and friends did not afford me an opportunity to be *seen*, let alone recognized. So I thought I was white on the outside. I felt drawn to black people that I found all around me. Yet I remained emotionally torn given the mixed bag of responses I would receive from both white and black people with whom I would try to connect. The very few times I felt safe was when I was speaking Spanish with my Puerto Rican friends who never seemed to make me feel uncomfortable in my own skin.

Kids are smart. I knew it when I was young and I know it now. If you are a parent reading this book, I am sure that you can recount many a time wherein you found your child mimicking a word or behavior that made you realize that your child understood things way beyond their years.

You can be sure that children see and feel it all. Children see the glances exchanged between parents during uncomfortable moments. Kids feel the energy in the atmosphere go from positive to negative when racial undertones are expressed in words or jokes. Hatred is sensed when slurs or stereotypical talk are expressed by unsuspecting or uncaring people either in person or on the television.

Children have a unique ability to understand ideas of value and meaning when it comes to others responding to the color of their skin. For those closest to them and from the onset of their racial identity development, parents, caregivers, extended family members and educators must be conscientious of race. They must be ready to confront the historical legacy of slavery and color as it affects the biracial children they are raising and impacting.

I will never forget the time when, suffering from early onset colorblindness, I took for granted all the amount of power that can fit into an ugly word. I found myself in a playful sort of verbal back and forth with a white girlfriend of mine who lived in one of the apartments near me. She was a friend that I played with often and one who would knock on my mother's door just to ask if I could come out and play.

We may have been seven or eight and I remember the escalation of emotion saddled to every word during our playful exchange. Words big and small that meant nothing to either of us were exchanged back and forth with the ease one would display while sitting in tandem on a see saw. At some point I remember becoming aware of the group of kids that had walked up and encircled us; the crowd growing larger and larger than had existed just moments before.

I recall my friend and I being very in tune with the excitement of the crowd and likewise, we adjusted our energies to match the ever-increasing tone of group. It wasn't long before our sense of playfulness subsided as each of us frantically tried to think of new, grown up words that would impress the onlookers and deliver an element of shock and surprise. At one point, I remember becoming caught up in the feeling of being so in tune with someone and the energy of the crowd while at the same time being hit with the realization that nothing I was saying was *getting* to my friend.

What she couldn't have known was that every word she was uttering was hurting me like never before. What I couldn't show was that she had struck a nerve about five words back and now the crowd was getting in on the momentum that she had picked up. I knew that I was close to tears but I wasn't ready to give in to defeat. I knew that if she or the other kids who were standing around saw me cry, I would lose my position on the playground in no time at all so I began to run through all of sorts of different scenarios in my mind.

I began to recall all of the things I had heard other people say and the names and words other kids had called me. Whether they lived in my neighborhood and had uttered these bad words while fighting or whether I recited them from an "R" rated television show that I would snuck to watch when my mother wasn't looking, no word was off limit. I tried frantically to produce words in time with the expectations of the excited bystanders.

Then I got it! I knew which word had hurt me the most; had made me run away in defeat, leaving me feeling dirty and ashamed. It was the same word that had garnered the most attention from a previous crowd and it was the same word that to date was unmatched in venom.

So I let the girl continue in her verbal assault and duly noted her frustration as I puffed up my chest as she went on and on calling me stupid, a zebra, a half-breed, and dog. I knew that she was running out of things to say but I kept my cool as the anticipation of the juvenile bystanders continued to grow. I let her finish and just as it began to quiet down, I let her have it.

With every fiber of hate in my being, I walked straight up to this ignorant girl's face, squared my shoulders and in the loudest voice I could muster, I called her a nigger. Though my mouth was empty I could feel my chest filling up with the weight of the word.

With a huge hole in my heart, the girl stepped back and pointed a bony white finger in my face and started to laugh. Everyone else began to laugh and point and I began to cry. I didn't know what I had just done but all of a sudden, I felt so bad and ashamed.

All the kids began to laugh and scream but they weren't laughing and screaming at her. They were pointing their words and fingers at me. Before I could turn and run home, the hole in my heart exploded and my body ached with heat and hurt.

When I raced into my house and my mother saw me crying, she asked what was wrong and what I had done. I couldn't even catch my breath long enough to tell her what had just happened or how I was feeling. There were no words left to describe the isolation and confusion that wracked every fiber of my being.

It took hours for my mother to get me to calm down and when I explained to her all of the events of this particular afternoon and the word that I had used, what stays with me today is the memory of the absence of words between me and my mother. That was it! My mother said nothing.

She sat there, holding me close as I cried. With no other priority revealing itself I remember her rocking me back and forth and back and forth. She rocked me until there were no more tears to come.

She rocked away the shame. She rocked away the hurt and the confusion. She held me and comforted me until I could breathe again.

She held me even closer until I could nod my head when she asked me if I was all right. I remember distinctly how tightly she held me as if the tighter she held me the higher the wall of protection would grow and build up around me. I remember sharing this moment with my mother and feeling like there was no other place for me in the world except right there in my mother's arms.

I am not sure how other parents would have handled this situation. But after I stopped crying and composed myself, I don't remember my mom saying anything else about the word that I used or the experience that I had. I do remember making the decision, almost a sort of oath to myself, that I would never use that word again ever in my life.

While I have never again used that word, I have continued to experience and discover its power. To this day, I have been confronted with the word hundreds of times. People have called me the word, described me using the word and I have heard it used in songs and in movies. I have even seen it written in novels and books that I was forced to read while attending school.

Even making the decision to use the word in this book was a very hard choice to make. But I need parents, caregivers, family members and educators to feel what I felt and hear what I heard. I need you to understand the power that the word possesses. It is only in this way, that I can express how unnatural it is for such an evil word to be used in any sort of attempt at endearment or inclusion.

I challenge all artists to tap into their creative juices to come up with a word or term that describes them from the inside out instead of as the world has seen them. I challenge people, people of color in particular, to step up to the plate and recognize your God given ability to forever alter how others perceive and receive you just by altering the way you think and feel about yourself. Manifest your ideal and you manifest all that is good and all that is perfect.

Assume an identity that is rooted in freedom and accept only mutual respect and acceptance in return. The prevalent use of the evil "N-word" in our history can forever be vanquished if we, each of us, makes it our responsibility to tap into our divine purpose and manifest in our daily lives all of the prosperity and peace that we are due. When we make this our daily priority, the Universe will respond with similar energy and action. With every word that we utter from our lips we are being called to a higher level of consciousness and responsibility. I challenge all of us to meet this higher level of learning, living and loving today and every day of our lives.

As you can imagine, this was a pivotal moment in my life. I felt it then, but I didn't understand it until years later. This moment, mirrored in thousands of multiracial homes, is an opportunity for learning, loving and growing.

As biracial children, we have the choice to give in to trying to make others feel the hatred and negativity that we are sometimes faced with. Parents, as our first line of defense, you have the choice to give the biracial community a freedom that, once instilled, will prevent biracial individuals from ever doubting that a choice exists again when confronted with an opportunity to make someone else feel love or hate.

Nine

Freedom Exists When You Know Who You Are

If we agree that parents, caregivers, family members and educators have a responsibility to provide a freedom to biracial children then it is fair to ask: how do they accomplish this task? Freedom is given by providing choices and options. Freedom is given by providing instruction and knowledge.

Freedom is given by providing unconditional love. Freedom is laying the groundwork so that your biracial children know how unique and remarkable they truly are. Freedom is providing them with the opportunity to make choices, based on inspired knowledge that will keep them at the forefront of expressing love, gratitude and understanding at all times.

The type of freedom that I am talking about is the freedom afforded by individuals who are self-aware and who are willing to provide biracial children with opportunities to experiment with self-expression. Biracial children develop identities and forms of self-expression on a daily basis and in response to changing ideas and experiences. People raising mixed race children must be conscious and aware of the freedom that they must give in order to allow biracial children to develop the limits and contents of their racial identity.

Adults must patiently stand by while biracial children test out and re-adjust their chosen identity in relation to all of the feelings, emotions and responses that they receive from their internal and external worlds. Parents of biracial children have to be ready to deal with the unique perceptions and differences that exist within the minds, bodies and hearts of mixed race children. They must be prepared to accept and receive a biracial child who manifests a different and distinct internal appearance from the physical appearance that is seen by the outside world.

A mixed race child may appear to the outside world as an individual with dark skin and yet this same child may identify racially with the perspective and nuances usually reserved for individuals who appear white to the outside world. On the inside, the child in this dilemma thinks, feels and expresses within a white frequency even though this child's physical appearance would be classified as black. People raising or interacting with mixed race children must be prepared to continually educate and prepare *themselves* to accept a biracial child's racial identity even when this identity receives challenges or objections by mainstream society.

As members of families and communities we must be aware of the opportunities that exist on a daily basis that allow us to respond to children and individuals who may not fit into our preconceived notions of race or identity. We must remain steadfast and understand the sheer power that our responses have when a biracial child is looking to each one of us to either reject or accept their behaviors and expressions. At the heart of our response is the ability to validate and reinforce a biracial child's chosen racial identity, which can exist in the external world as either connected to or apart from the child's network or sphere of influence.

There have been many instances wherein I have personally experienced situations where white parents raising biracial children, having no connection with or relationship to the parent of color, will outwardly deny the racial identity expressed by their child. After speaking with these parents it is clear that the parent is not comfortable with the racial connotation represented by the child's chosen race. Sometimes the parent left raising the child actually demonstrates actions and mentalities that would actually appear to punish the child for selecting a racial identity not understood or accepted by this parent.

As evidenced by my own upbringing, I learned very quickly how to turn my "blackness" on and off depending on whether my mother was present and watching. While full knowledge of my racial and cultural heritage wasn't granted to me until I was in my mid-twenties, during my childhood years I found myself taken with all things that my family and society considered black. I fell into an almost trance like state as I interacted on the fringes with the black kids in my school and the people of color that lived in my neighborhood.

Given my curious and competitive nature, I would follow other black girls around and listen as they spoke words of songs I had never heard and carried harmonies that my ears had never experienced. I would stare as I watched their bodies mimic something that I had seen on MTV but never dared dance to fearing some sort of admonishment from my mother. In the privacy of my bedroom I would try to mimic the words that they spoke and the tones and dialects of their voices when delivering a sentence or reciting words from a song.

I would try to copy their moves when dancing and I even tried to flip my hair as I saw these girls doing. The problem was that these young women of color had access to the source of culture and real life experiences in which all of their words, movements and beliefs were rooted. I had none.

If their mothers, sisters, and pop culture icons were their primary access point, I was learning and experiencing everything "black" from an access point that was 2-3 times removed from the source. I mean these girls had been hot combing, flat ironing and relaxing their hair for years. At the age of ten I still wore a picked out afro and had no idea that there existed chemicals that could make my hair do the same amazing things that I saw these girls do with their hair.

While there were a few instances that I would wonder why they didn't wear barrettes like I did, more times than not, I was more envious of their hairstyle and accessories than they were of mine. In fact, I don't recall any of them ever coming up to me to compliment me on any of the barrettes that my mother would put in my hair. Even though my mother to this day would argue this point with me, I am positively sure that I was not making a fashion statement among my peers.

My interaction with other black kids was very staccato. They would see me hanging around on the outskirts of their play time and whether I was invited in was always based on whether they needed someone to make fun of or to put down. So even if I were invited to play I would hesitate and take my time entering their group. I was never sure if they were serious or joking when they invited me to play and this hesitancy to interact with groups of women, white or black, remains with me today.

Given the interrupted glimpses into black life that I received during my first ten or eleven years of biracial life, I was always surprised by the amount of things that I was able to learn. While I was confident in my athletic abilities during this time in my life I was pleased and genuinely happy at the new abilities that seemed to jump out from just below the surface of my racial awareness when dancing or singing with the black girls who were, in some way, able to tolerate me. However, no matter how excited I ever became at learning a new dance move or being able to remove the whiteness from my voice enough to be able to sound like I was from where they were from, I knew that there was no way that I could ever share these endeavors or triumphs with my mother.

I saw how my mother responded to black women whose daughters danced in the lawns in our neighborhood and I never wanted her to look at me in that same way. While I would never categorize my mother as racist, I just knew that everything in the black world was very different from the world that she was from and the world in which I had convinced her I wanted to be in forever.

Until I was able to rationalize my mother's feelings and responses to blackness (which wouldn't be for many, many years to come) I wanted to receive all of my mother's love and acceptance that I could get for as long as I could get it. In moments like these, I feel that I lived a very dual life. In my white mother's presence, I did very white things. This was my norm and the life I was very comfortable with. But behind my mother's back, I began to crave the things I was seeing, hearing and feeling while hanging out with my black friends.

These things were so exotic to me and seemed so foreign that I always felt like I was being bad when I indulged. I know now that this is how I personally formed a connection in my own mind. I equated blackness with being bad; with something negative and something that should be punished.

Even today at the age of thirty-six, I find myself gauging certain behaviors and traits as bad or good based on whether they are something that my mother would approve of. This, in my opinion, is the bane of existence for the biracial individual. We find ourselves judged constantly. We are loved and hated and constantly judge ourselves while we try to rationalize love and hate.

This tiring process is based on the degree of the color of our skin and the experiences that we had with others in our lifetimes who were in a position to justify or nullify our behavior and outward appearance. The fact that some individuals will consciously, or unconsciously, deny the racial identity adopted by their biracial child says volumes more about the inability of these individuals to cope and develop their own understanding of racial identity than about the child's inability to grow and learn about themselves. This fact powerfully impacts the child's sense of racial identity.

If we accept that family is our first line of defense in the racial developmental onion analogy then we know that we are already working against societal notions based in white supremacy. From this foundational truth we can better analyze the overall process that seems to occur naturally when individuals, families, media and society begin to devalue blackness. Working from this framework, there should be no question that devaluation can and does thwart a biracial child's ability to reconsider and shift their racial identity when their chosen identity is challenged or rejected. "In fact, validation or rejection of one's chosen racial identity contributes greatly to the overall wellness of mixed-race people. Irrespective of the identity mixed-race people construct, the degree of validation or rejection they experience from others, especially those who are emotionally significant to them, can either reinforce their self-understanding and support a sense of identity cohesion, or can undermine their sense of self and create psychic distress."[11]

PART THREE
<u>Color Blind</u>
<u>A Mixed Girl's Perspective on Biracial Life</u>

Ten
<u>Racial Identity Development: The Role of the Schools</u>

Based on the make up of most of our communities, the next onion layer that we have to consider when discussing the process of biracial identity development would have to be the schools. A child's educational setting and experience is the second most important factor that influences the racial identity development of biracial children. It is within the school setting that children learn how to relate and interact with other persons of similar ages, mentalities and resources.

As individuals raising or impacting the lives of biracial children, are you familiar with the racial "goings on" that exist in your child's school? What rating would your child's school receive if the racial climate of each classroom were measured? Are you familiar with the racial composition of your child's school and classrooms? How about the racial composition of their friends and peers?

If you were observing your child in action during a typical school day how would you describe your child's ability to flourish within multicultural frameworks? Would you be able to recognize when your child was actually operating within the defined margins that exist between cultures, religions and color lines? While learning and playing, how often is your child being forced to reject any part of their racial identity?

Are your biracial children forced to re-evaluate how they identify with children of other races in order to feel accepted or wanted by and amongst their peers? Does the school that your children attend acknowledge a need for a conversation on race? Are the school administrators and educators taking a proactive stance when it comes to creating or fostering ra-racial awareness and celebrating diversity?

Does the school provide sensitivity training to its personnel? What ongoing opportunities exist for teachers to learn new ideologies that promote healthy racial awareness, behaviors and attitudes? Is there a healthy track record of teachers being aware and mindful of how their blatant and/or covert biases, attitudes and behaviors affect children?

Do you believe the answers to these questions will have any bearing on your biracial child's educational experience? Depending on how you answered these questions the actual implications may surprise you. You may not yet be aware of how and why biracial children end up identifying with and emulating the characteristics of the racial group with which they interact, exchange ideas and experiences.

Authors Rockquemore and Laszloffy explain studies that suggest that if your child's school is predominantly white then mixed race children will pick up characteristics and behaviors of their predominantly white peers and begin to value these characteristics more. Furthermore, studies suggest that this adaptation is clear cut across all racial lines: within most settings and environments, biracial children will begin to align themselves with the dominantly represented race, especially when this situation is found within the school setting. The same arrangement of adaptation is seen when the school environment or setting is found to be predominantly black. Mixed race children will pick up characteristics, behaviors and attitudes of their black peers. "In other words, they become comfortable among those who they see and interact with daily. Whether it is a white child in a black environment or a black child in a white environment, children adapt to their surrounds."[12]

One of the most detailed memories I have about my middle school experience is closely aligned with my body image and the clothing that my mother would find for me to wear. Between the ages of ten to twelve I was in the fifth and seventh grades. I stood about 5'7" and weighed about 125 lbs. I was tall and slender for my age to say the least.

While most of the boys in my neighborhood wanted me to be on their team whether we were playing basketball, football or tag, I never fit in with the girls. Whether it was the condition of my hair or the style of my clothes, the girls in my class and my neighborhood would torment me daily. I remember rising every morning and having to make a selection from clothes that never seemed to actually fit my frame.

And of course I was still using a pik to pick out my mini afro so the jokes were always on me. The one and only time my mother tried doing something with my hair was while she was in cosmetology school. She enrolled in cosmetology school after my sister had completed her first year. Needless to say, while talented black women who aspired to own their own beauty salons surrounded my mom and my sister, I became my mother's cute, tall guinea pig for everything and anything having to do with hair.

My sister gave me my first relaxer, which allowed me to see my visions of long flowing hair realized, even though this length lasted for only about a month. My hair got shorter and shorter as my sister and mother practiced trimming split ends and roller setting my thick, mixed head of hair. Before my mother graduated, my mother began practicing buzz cuts and I seemed to have no say in how short was too short. As you can imagine, my hair, and subsequently, my body image and sense of self, was never something I ever felt in control of during the years when it mattered most.

So here I was, in middle school, trying to test out this very athletic body of mine while marveling at the fashions worn by all of the popular girls around me. I saw other tall girls with huge breasts and shorter girls with very flat chests. Then there were the popular girls who seemed to have it all: the perfect body (or at least the body most admired by boys) and a large number of people trying to be their friend.

I remember sitting quietly in awe as I would listen to these girls trade stories about how far they had to travel to the mall so their mothers could pick out designer shoe this and designer jacket that. I was waiting to hear from a single one of these girls that they too had to wait for their mothers to coordinate schedules with another girl's mother in order to go pick up clothes that the other girl had out grown. I never did hear other girls having this conversation.

I was never known in school as the popular girl or the girl who attracted the most stares from the boys. No, I was the girl who was known for showing up with her hair in a mess. Flat on one side and puffy and picked out on the other; wearing tight pants that were too short with black shoes that left black marks all over the gym floor.

On top of all this, my mother was into this whole, "you are not going to go to school looking like all of those other girls" mode. So unlike the other girls who were sporting Jordache jeans and whatever sneaker was "in" during those days, I was wearing tight fitting dress pants with small heeled dress shoes, blouses (do we even use that word anymore) and dress jackets.

I know in her mind, every day she sent me off to school, she probably saw me coming home with a story that sounded something like, "and while I was walking home, you dressed me so well that a big, black limo pulled over and this very professional looking man got out and told me how much I stood out from everyone else. He knows I'm young and all but he wants me to come to work for him and he offered me a lot of money". I'm sure it went something like that in my mother's head. I am also sure that she never understood that the reason I was fighting and crying and suffering in school so much was because of how she dressed me.

And there was no easy way for a girl like me, constantly feeling caught in the middle, to dress. The white girls had their fashion trends and the black girls had theirs. Just from looking at me, one would assume I existed outside of and away from the same trends that were influencing everyone else's lives.

Given the way my mother chose to dress me I felt isolated and alone. Add to this out of touch picture a large, unmanageable afro, barrettes and ill fitting shoes and you would arrive at the outward appearance that I portrayed to the very cruel world. If I were on the outside looking in, I probably wouldn't be able to see past this unmade image either. Even at the age of eleven or twelve, I understood why neither the black girls nor the white girls would accept me or want to have anything to do with me.

So what do my school day experiences mean to other biracial girls? What do my experiences say about the state of interracial experiences within school systems? In general, maybe my school age experiences mean nothing. Then again, like most biracial children, my school age experiences are the ones that come to mind every time I hear someone talking about kids today having the newest fashions and technology. They are the memories I immediately go back to when I see news reports about kids bullying one another. My school age experiences are what prepared me for the brutality I would experience from the adults that kids eventually become.

During these years, I never heard the word desegregation. I never heard adults or teachers referring to their efforts or programs as having anything to do with the integration of races. I do remember that the talk on the playground would revolve around who lived where, what kind of clothes kids were wearing and the makes and models of the cars their parents were driving.

Unlike the discussions on education that take place today wherein the resumes of educators and school leaders are hashed out and reviewed, school days for me while in the sixth and seventh grade were personal and had everything to do with the color of my skin, the size of my hair and the quality (or lack thereof) of the hand me down clothes that I wore on a daily basis. Again, I point you to an excerpt written by Eduardo Bonilla-Silva in his book, Racism Without Racists where he provides insight into the failures of integrated school systems (such as the one that I attended in my middle school years) to respond to the issue of colorblindness as an ideology that pervades our schools:

> *"Why is it that integrated schools have not provided a meaningful platform for interracial contacts? First, the structure of 'desegregated' schools is such that interracial interactions do not lead to significant cross-racial relationships. For instance, even when whites are bused to predominantly minority schools, tracking guarantees they have a mostly white experience in their schools. Case in point: almost all of our respondents described their classes (academic track) as 'mostly white,' even in cases where*

the schools were described as 40 percent or more minority! Our respondents also rarely remembered being in classes or clubs in which students of color were the majority. Second, school integration typically occurs late in the lives of whites (usually in high school). By that time, they have already developed emotional attachments to whites as their primary social group, learned a number of stereotypes about minorities, and bypassed the development of the skills necessary to navigate multicultural situations." [13]

The key to understanding this very complicated onion layer that represents our schools and educational systems is best seen and explained when we look at the knowledge and personal experiences of the people responsible for leading our schools. These are the key individuals who are responsible for setting the tone for the parents and children in any given educational setting. The tone that is eventually set will impact the way situations of racial discord and tension are perceived, handled and explained.

Having said this, most of the comments I experienced during my middle school years came from the other kids around me. These comments and jabs made a great impression on me and forced me to question the color of my skin as it related to the skin color of my mother and my peers. However, it should be noted that these comments were made in front of my teachers and I remember how curious these teachers appeared while awaiting my response.

Instead of saying or doing anything that would make a bullying child stop, the teachers just stood there...waiting...to see how I would respond...waiting to hear the answer that I would give. It's as if they too wanted to hear my response when the other kids were egging me on, calling me names and yelling at me to tell them who my father was or demanding that I pick a white or black side. The looks on the teachers faces, the words slipping from the kid's mouths, the silence as the teachers waited to hear my answer, all of these things reinforced for me that there was a conspiracy going on and everyone around me, even the older kids I didn't know, knew more about me, who my father was, and why I wasn't getting any truth from my mother, than I did.

As one can see, within a school setting, there is power and knowledge in operating at the far, opposite end of the color blind spectrum. Instead of pretending not to see race or racial stereotypes and prejudices, parents will ultimately serve their children better if they are aware of some key elements and factors that should and should not be operating within their children's schools. If you care about the external environment that has almost as much influence over the racial identity development of your children as the role of family, then be prepared to gather information about the best school for your children. Authors Rockquemore and Laszloffy suggest parents spend time considering the following forms of questions:

1. *Does the school or school administration enhance racial understanding in an open environment?*

2. *Is there open dialogue between teachers and the administration and children and teachers?*

3. *Is race being discussed in the classroom?*

4. *Are minority faculty members being sought after?*

5. *Are teachers unconsciously submitting children of color for more severe disciplinary action than their white counterparts?*

6. *Is the racial climate of the school being studied to find room for improvement and opportunities for discussion?*

Based on the answers to these questions, can you tell if your mixed-race child would thrive within the school they currently attend or are going to attend? How will the other students and overall tone of the school's administration affect your child's sense of self? Would you be comfortable entering the school in order to talk race and race relations as it relates to your child? [14]

Eleven

Racial Identity Development: The Role of Friends and Peers

As we continue the discussion about the racial identity development of biracial children, we find ourselves approaching the outermost layer of our developmental onion. This external layer signifies the role of friends and peers as they relate to the racial identity development of biracial children. Friends and peers can have similar effects on our children in two extreme ways.

For as many instances of positive support, encouragement and discovery that can result from a friendship or an association, the opposite amount of negative interactions and experiences can exist and cause even more damage than the positive influences. Through their interactions with friends and peers, mixed-race children learn to challenge, accept and re-define their racial identities to the world. Acceptance from these outside forces can teach our children to become comfortable in their own skin and make them willing to share experiences, secrets, shelter and support.

Likewise, unhealthy relationships with these same outside forces can strip biracial children of any pre-conceived notions they may have developed regarding ethics and standards. With the loss of this comfort zone, multiracial children may begin to act out, become emotionally frail and insecure, ultimately sabotaging the relationships they once held dear. "Ideally, all children, and mixed-race children in particular, would have access to a racially diverse group of peers. A diverse peer group allows greater opportunity to develop a multifaceted view of race and

79

expands children's options in terms of their own racial identity." [15]

Rockquemore and Laszloffy suggest that parents conduct a racial assessment of their children's friendships and offer the following questions to begin the process of evaluating their children's friendships and the role race may play:

1. *Does your child seek out relationships with a racially diverse group of friends?*

2. *How much open dialogue occurs between your child and her/his friends about race? What is the overall theme and tone of the dialogue? If no such dialogue occurs, why?*

3. *How dependent does your child seem to be on receiving approval or validation from her/his friends? How might matters of race be related to this?*

4. *Do your child's friendships (either overtly or covertly) discourage them from acknowledging and expressing any parts of their racial identity?*

5. *Are you aware of any tensions in your children's friendships that may be racially based? If yes, how are these tensions handled?*

6. *Have you noticed sudden shifts in your child's moods and behaviors that may indicate some underlying distress (e.g., becoming unusually sullen, quiet, withdrawn, angry, moody, irritable, and/or distracted, a drop in grades, marked changes in daily routines and/or personal care activities, a sudden, noticeable*

decrease or increase in interactions with friends)? If yes, what types of factors might explain the changes? Could racial issues be related to this at all?

7. *Do the parents of your child's friends make racist or racially insensitive comments, expressing racially biased attitudes? Do they behave in racially biased ways?*

If parents find that, after conducting the suggested evaluation listed above, race may be responsible for shaping how their children initiate or retain friendships, they should be ready to assess the friends, relationships and context of the identified stressors; step in and create an environment wherein the children feel comfortable discussing any concerns or issues; and communicate a sensitivity and understanding to the child's plight. [16]

There were so many times in my early childhood when I wanted my mother to push me. I wanted her to push me and ask me just one more question. But her fear and the existence of her unresolved issues would not allow her to acknowledge what was really going on in my life with regard to race, my friends and my experiences.

Unlike the holes in my emotional relationships during my pre-teen years, my bedroom in our apartment had it all: a chest full of baby dolls and all of the pieces of the Barbie California mansion that a little girl could ever want. Before I discovered the freedom of the playground or the anonymity of the woods, other kids would love to play with me in my bedroom and I loved that they wanted to play with me.

It wasn't until the age of eight or ten that my play dates with our neighbor girls began to intrude on the sense of safety that my room afforded to me. While I was comfortable playing with whatever dolls I had been given, these other girls began to question me as to why I wasn't playing with a black baby doll. Well now what was I supposed to say to that?

All of my Barbie dolls and baby dolls were white. My mother was telling me all the time that I wasn't black, so why would I play with a black baby doll? Every time this happened I would leave the safety of my bedroom and travel down our set of wooden stairs, making a beeline to the comfort of my mother's lap where I would try to ask my mother about something one of the girls had just said.

I would huddle up to her and intertwine my arms with hers and lean into her. She would put her head on top of my head and wrap her arms around me and when she asked me what I needed or if everything was ok, I wouldn't say anything remotely close to what I had come to ask her about. There was something about being that close to my mother: feeling her and smelling her and knowing that she loved me. I felt that I would mess all of this up if I dared to ask something so stupid about why I didn't have a black baby doll to play with.

So I didn't push the subject and she never pushed back. We both went on our meandering ways, ignorant to the possibilities of what mentioning the unmentionable could have unleashed: the freedom it could have given both of us and the rich history I could have inherited. Instead, I would slide down her lap and climb the stairs once again, all the while conversing with my mixed little mind saying, "Haven't we already been through this enough times?"

My mind would begin to shift into automatic and I would begin to remember all of the details of all of the times that my mother had taken me through all of the photo albums and shown me my dark skinned, Hungarian uncle. His light green eyes would stare back at me from a photo that was seared into my mind. The thickness of his lips would capture my imagination as I saw his image in the photos begin to move, his eyes capturing my gaze as his lips parted and an unmelodic Hungarian verse floated to my ears.

His words reinforced the stories told to me by my mother during nights when the hurt of the day escaped from my body through energetic tears that raced toward an unseen finish line. Every day I was torn. I was torn by all of the hints that my friends and peers were giving me. I was torn by the history lesson that my mother had already given me.

What I knew felt good on a daily basis was my mother holding me and loving me. So, in the end, while growing up, I chose to take my mother's side and believe more in what she was telling me and showing me versus what my friends were only courageous enough to suggest with the words that they had at their disposal.

Twelve
Boarding School and the Real World:
A Story of Racial Extremes

It goes without saying that understanding how race plays a factor in the overall development of biracial children's racial identity is a fundamental need for all parents, educators, family members and caregivers. This understanding goes beyond knowing the breakdown of racial figures of any given school. This understanding even surpasses the ability of parents to know, to any certain degree, the heritage and nationalities of their children's friends and peers. [17]

Given my personal interactions with individuals on the basis of race, it is my opinion that we need to change our entire mentality about race relations and our understanding of racial identity development. The possibility that a healthy and accepting racial environment could exist first struck me when I was accepted into an all girls' college preparatory boarding school in Northeast Ohio. Here I was, a tall, athletic mixed girl from Ashtabula, Ohio surrounded by other girls who spoke little or no English, hailed from far away places like Tanzania, Mexico, Korea, Germany, Spain, Japan and Tasmania, and yet were very confident in who they were as young women.

During my five year stay at boarding school, I marveled at the emphasis that was placed on celebrating one another's cultural and ethnic differences. For the first time in my life I experienced people who used more than words derived from colors to describe what they were about and how they saw themselves in the world at large. There was meaning behind every relationship and a curiosity that led us to learning everything we could about one another.

Boarding school was a storybook place. During winter months we would trek over a campus covered in snow. The white landscape broken only by the stoic, red brick buildings that sat nestled on a sprawling 365-acre campus. Our campus maintained a sense of wonder as horse trails intertwined with lacrosse fields and pedestrian paths carved their way through a wooded dorm circle that allowed on campus students to traverse the grounds between administration buildings and their mansion like dorms.

At the age of thirteen I walked onto this campus and at that moment, I tapped into a freedom that allowed me to express the thoughts in my head and the songs in my heart without having to worry about whether someone was looking at me and wondering "what is she?" For the first time in my life I found myself fitting in with all sorts of unknown colors and hues. Hair textures were short, long, wavy, straight, curly, natural and processed. There were tall girls, short girls, skinny girls and chubby girls.

Within this eclectic mix I found my voice. I excelled in the classrooms and even more on the athletic fields where I found myself competing in volleyball, basketball, softball and lacrosse. I learned to ride horses, speak Japanese, perfected my Spanish and learned how to keep score in tennis.

At boarding school I found a place where I was sought after for my opinion and praised for the way I recited a poem. I competed with the best in the academic world and was able to travel to Ontario, Canada and Niagara for the sole purpose of seeing a play or listening to exotic music. I learned the art of debate and was honored to watch young women grow and learn in spirit and in mind. Gone were the public school, girly competitions that found me praying for a designer hand me down in the bag of used clothes my mother would pick up for me from her friend's home. Gone were the days when I was laughed at because I didn't know something that someone thought I should just because of the color of my skin.

The world I entered at boarding school provided me with solutions, choices and information on the very same issues that just a year before would have plagued my soul. No more did I feel the need to barricade myself in my bedroom, away from my color blind mother, in order to cry out all of the built up frustration that seemed to find its way into every crack and crevice of my starving soul. For the first time, as I remembered the nights I spent staring into the mirror in my mother's bathroom, asking God, "why?" I had an answer.

I was praised and accepted for the inherent things that made me different from my educated peers. Beautiful girls told me for the first time that they thought I was pretty. They even asked if they could play with my hair; the same hair that caused me shame and earned me nothing but heartache. Besides the times when my mother would hold me and try to soothe my screams of confusion and frustration after having been attacked by the newest bully on our block, boarding school was the first time I felt loved by other people who saw me for me and seemed to like what they saw.

This fairytale of love and peace lasted for five wonderful years and during this time, I learned what it was like to be a woman with a voice in a society that didn't always want to hear from a woman who had a voice and knew how to use it. Attending boarding school, specifically, an all girls' boarding school gave me courage and empowered me to have faith in myself before and above anyone else. For all of the years that I spent searching for someone else to believe in, I had, for the first time, been taught that I could become the answer to my own questions and the solution to any and all of the problems that I created.

Like most young girls in high school, I couldn't wait to enter the real world and flex my "me, me, me" muscle. At eighteen, I was set to go to college and devour all that it had to offer me. And if being mixed while attending boarding school was AWESOME, then being a mixed girl from a small town who had attended boarding school and who was now going to college was AMAZING!

I found myself wanted by whites and blacks, girls and boys. All of sudden I had so many friends that I didn't know what to do with myself. Having learned Japanese and "proper" Spanish allowed me to interact with a whole new crowd and my college prep experience enabled me to access the college classroom without fear and quite a bit of confidence in my abilities and capabilities.

Once I graduated from college and was forced to enter the "real world" the longing to return to my boarding school days took me over completely. I would dream of returning to the campus that comforted even the smallest amount of racial anxieties. I longed for the population of individuals who allowed me to feel free to be and experiment with who I thought I was or wanted to be.

After graduation I moved back home to Ashtabula for a brief time before moving to Cleveland, Ohio with my best friend Lenita who I had met while modeling in Erie, Pennsylvania. Outwardly and physically we were total opposites and yet we clicked in a way that was totally unexpected. We came from different worlds and experienced the same world in very, very different ways. And through it all Lenita, in all of our many adventures, never once asked me to compromise any part of my racial identity to make her feel comfortable.

We lived together and found work at the same company together. It was within this corporate insurance environment that I again began to struggle with all of the hopes and naïveté that a mixed girl could possibly have. I found myself surrounded by white trainers and supervisors who cared nothing about the things that had previously made me extraordinary.

To me it felt like it was easier for these white individuals to place me into a category with every other black person that surrounded me instead of trying to deal with me as a biracial individual. They seemed so confused when they heard me speak and saw the way I interacted with callers on the phone. I excelled within their training frameworks and yet they refused to see me as an equal.

Instead, they found every opportunity to tell me why I couldn't advance and why I had to wait my turn (all the while referencing examples from my black counterparts). Without emphasizing the issue of race I tried to make the case (while referencing examples of my white counterparts) that I too was excelling in areas of training and deserved to be acknowledged as well. I explained in the best way that I knew how that my educational background demanded excellence and that was exactly what I was prepared to give.

It didn't matter. To these white managers and supervisors there was no room for advancement for me- a woman of color. They had their stereotypes and expectations and I was to operate within these confines. What they and my black counterparts failed to tell me was that there was this thing called a status quo that I had yet to be taught about.

I was to learn my role and maintain myself within these preset boundaries. Boundaries that made my white and black co-workers feel comfortable. Well, there was a reason that I had never heard about the status quo. And so I fought them. I fought them all tooth and nail. I fought everything about the divide that I felt.

When I started the insurance job I was twenty-two years old. As soon as I realized how much my perceived race was being used against me, I really felt like I had walked into a "them versus me" situation. I saw and felt the looks that the white managers gave to my colleagues and me. I also saw and heard the comments my black coworkers made around me, behind my back and in front me.

Everyone it seemed was beginning to challenge my racial identity. In fact, we all saw it and felt it but I seemed to be the only one who wanted to talk about it. I wanted to scream at everyone, "Don't you know I'm biracial?" I wanted to shake my white managers and yell, "Stop treating me like I'm black". Likewise, I wanted to shake my black coworkers and yell, "Stop treating me like I'm white".

From this point on in my life, my differences would no longer be something that was in my favor. In fact, I began to get a lot of challenges from black individuals even more than from the white individuals who were interviewing me, teaching me and in most cases, in the positions of power or influence in which I wanted to operate. Never before had I felt so different and not wanted.

Which brings me back to Lenita. Beautiful, brown skinned Lenita: confident in her blackness and in her beauty. While we played the game of life together we learned to cover for one another and supported each another. Lenita proved to be the one constant in my life that supported me and celebrated me. Lenita taught me to be comfortable in my own skin and she taught me about the value of being biracial.

Because of Lenita I learned that it was ok to be light skinned. She introduced me to Spike Lee and explained the racial divide that existed within the black sororities in the south. Lenita had the answers to most, if not all of my questions about life, men and relationships. Unlike most of the people in my life, she had a lot of patience with me. There were many times that my questions would reveal a total lack of understanding or knowledge of how something worked or was used to playing out in the black community.

Without judgment or hesitation, my best friend would step up and "take me to school" and teach me about the very essence of my blackness. To this day she remains a sister to me. We have endured the unspeakable and have shared the unmentionables. I doubt that she knows how much of an impact her friendship, acceptance and instruction meant to me while I was at such a vulnerable and crucial developmental stage in my early adult life. In fact, without the calm and support she provided, Tiffany Rae as you are experiencing or learning about her, wouldn't be half of who she is had it not been for Lenita

Thirteen
Colorblindness: The New Racism?

All of these experiences have been a small peek into some of the times in my life, when I was introduced to the power that color plays in our society. I know that my family's situation was not so unique that other biracial individuals, their families and friends, weren't also having them. What I do know is that all of the research I have done in order to help others have discussions on race and racial identity has led me to understand that not a lot of people are comfortable discussing race.

While it has become important to understand my own journey as a biracial individual I now realize that a lot of biracial people are **not** telling their stories. With the election of a mixed-raced man to the office of The President of the United States of America you would think that our country's discussion on race would continue without judgment and fear. Given the recent celebration of certain things "mixed" in Hollywood one would assume that there would be a surge in the interest in the number of families raising children mixed with colors and ethnicities that, not too long ago, were forbidden, looked down upon and discouraged.

I have found that this is not the case. These recent and trendy occurrences have not quieted the inner angst that mixed children feel when presented to the world by parents who have become color blind. So color blind in fact that they have taken away their child's very own ability to identify with and express the very remarkable traits that make them so different and so very unique. "Whether you are black or white, and irrespective of your stage of racial identity development, everyone internalizes some aspects of societal messages that overvalue whiteness and devalue blackness. The extent to which such messages are either deconstructed and rejected, or absorbed and integrated, shapes how a person comes to think and feel about their racial identity."[18]

One of the definitions of racism is summarized as any attitude, belief, behavior, or institutional arrangement that favors one racial group over another. Based on this definition, parents want to search and find the raging, obvious bigot shouting racial epithets at or around their biracial children. It appears that most parents and family members fail to see or acknowledge all of the quiet acts of racism found in every family, every community and every school.

Rarely do we see the hooded group, protesting with signs and burning crosses in front lawns. My generation appears to have already forgotten the "shotgun diplomacy at the voting booth". [19] But how many times have you heard about or witnessed the minority family being steered away from the neighborhood of their choice by a realtor or homeowner who just doesn't think that this community is the right place for this non-conforming family? How many brilliant, black scholars do you know who have interviewed for a high paying job only to be offered a very low paying job with no opportunity for mobility up the corporate ladder? [20]

Even in this globally diverse world, racism, prejudices and stereotyping still exists, just in different and various forms. If you find it hard to identify the act of racism in these examples, consider the parent who I encounter during workshops and presentations that can't wait to come up to me and declare the pledge they have made against racism. They go to lengths to describe the actions they have undertaken in order to remove the possibility of the theoretical racist or bigoted person from entering their lives or the lives of their children.

Parents raising biracial children are carefully choosing multiethnic friends and culturally diverse play dates. What is their goal? To help their biracial children understand that differences do, in fact, exist.

Yet these same parents can't seem to make the connection that being color blind can be just as powerful and negative as all of the examples listed above. Color blind people, that is to say, individuals who refuse to see the color of a person's skin as significant, end up doing just as much harm to their mixed-race children. By refusing to acknowledge the cultural and racial legacy that is associated with the color of their child's skin, color blind parents are in fact, denying their children the chance to understand, identify and celebrate the very essence of who they are and who they could eventually become. "...the insistence that we are 'color blind' is particularly problematic because it represents a false assessment of our attitudes, a refusal to acknowledge that we all harbor prejudicial beliefs as a result of living in America, and it provides a convenient pass for not doing the hard work of critically evaluating our own beliefs and behaviors." [21]

Take for instance the white parent who is raising a biracial child. As was the case with my own mother, most white parents continue to demonstrate patterns of behavior that keep them interacting with their white counterparts. Every day of their lives, these white parents continue to reinforce associations and relationships with other white people.

By reinforcing these relationships and associations, they are in essence reinforcing their sense of racial solidarity with other white people. It is during these times that preconceived notions held by other whites (those individuals not in charge of raising biracial children) can be communicated or reinforced. Some of these preconceived notions reinforce negatively held stereotypes of black people or other people of color.

Now in order to be fair and to show that I am not naïve in my understanding or acceptance of the fact that this process can, in fact, happen in reverse, I do state that these same phenomena can and do occur in the lives and households of black parents raising biracial children and parents of other cultures and other racial backgrounds. However, given the pervasiveness of white supremacy I offer the following as written by Eduardo Bonilla-Silva:

> *"The central component of any dominant racial ideology is its frames or set paths for interpreting information. These set paths operate as cul-de-sacs because after people filter issues through them, they explain racial phenomena following a predictable route. Although by definition dominant frames must misrepresent the world (hide the fact of dominance), this does not mean that they are totally without foundation. (For instance, it is true that people of color in the United States are much better off today than at any other time in history. However, it is also true-facts hidden by color-blind racism-that because people of color still experience systematic discrimination and remain appreciably behind whites in many important areas of life, their chances of catching up with whites are very slim. Dominant racial frames, therefore, provide the intellectual road map used by rulers to navigate the always rocky road of domination and derail the ruled from their track to freedom and equality."* [22]

In my own life, I did not flourish when I was denied the truth. My own mother's inability to see my color robbed me of an opportunity (and hence a freedom) to embrace my unique characteristics and understand the cultural heritage that would ultimately define an inherent part of who and what I am. Even today, my mother and I find that we discuss issues that affect the white and black community. Sometimes our perspectives are similar and sometimes they are very, very different.

Only now, through the open relationship that we have, does our dialogue reveal to me the frame that my mother used and uses to deal and interact with her family, her friends and me. I can see now how many of my mother's friendships during my childhood may have influenced or affected her beliefs about what it was to be white and what it was to be black. One of the most telling revelations for me was seeing who my mother was getting her information from.

My mother will readily admit that aside from the relationship she had with my biological father that produced me, she had no real "in" or connection to the black community. This is not to say that she was not seeking out information that would have helped her to raise me. However it is interesting to me to know that had she been interested in learning how to do my hair or have a conversation about race with me, her biracial daughter, she would have learned this from her white counterparts who may or may not have had experience raising biracial children.

Knowing what I know now, I know that she was the only one of her friends and family to be in the predicament of raising a child of color. My mother's predicament while raising me also raises another issue that is discussed later in this book. This very same network, while reinforcing any preconceived

97

notions of race, has the same power and potential to reinforce my mother's feelings about my father that she may have created based on the status of their relationship.

Like so many single parents today who find themselves separated, divorced or no longer involved with the other parent, suffice it to say, my mother had feelings about the man who provided half of my DNA. Whether her feelings were anger, hatred or acceptance, my mother will find "backup" or reinforcement of her feelings from her monoracial network. We know now that my mother's network happened to be a collection of all white people.

I often wonder if my mother's opinion about my father would have been different had a person of color been included in her inner circle. Would the communication gap be smaller had there been someone who understood black culture or someone who had a connection with other people in my father's community? Would there have at least been dialogue between my mother and father from the time I was conceived until the time I was in my mid to late twenties?

Would my mother have had an outlet to discuss or at least get rid of any or all of the negative feelings that she ended up harboring for so many years? And having had an opportunity to release this element of negativity, would my mother have been able to interpret, deal with and move on and forward in other relationships (platonic and romantic)? Would she have been able to provide me with access to my blackness and insight into my cultural heritage?

When I think of all the things that I eventually missed and all of the things that I was never able to talk about, I get sad. Against the advice of many progressives who are in tune with their "now" and all about releasing oneself from a past or a future, I find it hard to sever my ego and my heart from all of the "what ifs" that surround me and live inside of me. So many things about me would have been different had I merely known the true reason for my darker skin or my curly hair.

Had I simply been given the name and location of my father when I was twelve instead of twenty-six, I would have had the choice and freedom to do something about my future. But never having the choice; never feeling that sort of freedom affected me for the rest of my life by limiting my belief and understanding of how concepts of choice and freedom really worked. In fact, it wasn't until I found myself living and thriving at boarding school that I found myself free to discuss, for the very first time, the nuances of race, color, the historical legacies of relevant cultures and different types of cultural, racial and personal slaveries.

While engaged in conversations with other young women I found my heart fluttering and my mind racing. I was eager to obtain and digest even the smallest piece of information that would explain all of the missing tidbits of my life and allow it all to make sense. I would hang on every word hoping for someone to say something that would provide me with a mental road map that would set me on my way to my father. I was hungry for the smallest piece of advice, information or insight that I believed would help to restore me and give me back all of the small pieces that would eventually turn me into a person that felt whole and complete.

As I began to gain insight into other people's blackness, I began to inherit a sense of hatred for all of those people who had surrounded me in my life prior to boarding school. I pictured these people, in their basements holding secret meetings, devising ways to keep me in the dark and protect secrets that, if ever brought to the light, would hurt my mother, my sister and my father, with no regard for my feelings or me. I began to sense the unfairness that existed in the fact that all of these small pieces that had the potential to complete me were actually being held up and controlled by so many other people in my life.

Eventually, "all of these other people" ended up taking the form, color and shape of my mother who I began holding personally responsible for all of the mixed up feelings and emotions I was having about being her daughter. Unlike other teenagers who act out by using drugs or alcohol or being promiscuous, I acted out with a desire to shed the very skin that connected me in any way to my mother or my sister. During my five years at boarding school, I began to re-create my earlier years. I inserted people, places and conversations, which provided me with a picture, albeit a distorted one, of who I was and gave me a reason for being where I was at that time in my life.

If you thought my imagination had been at work during my adolescent years when I would envision famous R&B singers coming into town to claim me, than you would be astonished at the inner workings that occurred in my mind when I was separated from the one person who had previously been responsible for defining and reinforcing my whiteness. In these years, I explored the freedom I had to relish in new personas. I became alive in the knowledge that if I never again mentioned my connections to a white mother and a white life then no one would ever associate me with white ever again.

I tasted the freedom of assumed knowledge. I created elaborate images of myself in future positions of power; engaged in creative dramas with other powerful people. I colored my world beautiful and, looking back, my imaginary world was so full of color that there was not a stain of whiteness to be found.

As I sit and write this book, I have tried to figure out which of these two extremes played the biggest role in my ability to have created the future (that was then) that I find myself living today. Was it the separation of all color from birth to twelve or the obsequious blast of color that dominated the thoughts of my future after I entered boarding school? Either way, what has become my future, the life I am now living, is full of colorful days and diverse individuals.

For the first time, with the creation of my biracial coaching business and with the writing of this book, I have been able to rationalize the two most important extremes of my life. From my experience of living for so long in the margins of the pages of other people's lives, I have found a place in this world for me and for other biracial people just like me. For the first time, I am relishing in the freedom that comes from taking a stance and making a choice to remain grounded in every experience that has contributed to the way that I feel about my blackness and about my whiteness.

I have chosen to not fret about the entire "goings on" that occurred in the "in between". Rather, I am living there and accepting it. I am now empowered with answers and able to provide solutions. I am now in control of my future and directing all of my resources, gifts, talents and abilities. Instead of severing those very things that once made me feel so different and isolated, I have now embraced my uniqueness and I choose to celebrate my innate traits and characteristics in order to lead a more remarkable and purpose filled life.

As human beings, as children, as biracial individuals, we all need the small pieces that, in some cases, remain missing for far too long. In fact, we should be given these pieces one piece at a time during our formative years so that we can play with them, see how they fit and eventually, choose another piece to work with if we need to. It is only through this process that we will find ourselves able to grow mentally, emotionally and spiritually and transform from adolescents, through teenage years and into adulthood with a road map of truth.

By following this road map, we will be able to engage with all of the layers of our developmental onion. As we navigate the truths of our lives we will experience a journey that will eventually mold the ideas, perceptions and opinions that will ultimately provide us with a racial identity that best fits our personality. In this way, our puzzle will be personal and will be filled with the pieces that represent our unique biracial traits and characteristics.

PART FOUR

Color Blind

A Mixed Girl's Perspective on Biracial Life

Fourteen
Racial Identity Development and Skin: Why We Have Been Forced to Pick Sides

As we continue to discuss a biracial individual's racial identity development our picture would not be complete if we didn't take into consideration the very skin of the onion. Whether your onion is yellow, white or reddish purple, you have a translucent and permeable skin. The skin can at times, appear fresh or worn but no matter the travels it has seen, the onion skin comes with a certain toughness and vulnerability.

It is this skin that is first seen by people who are on the outside. These people walk around and have a choice as to whether they will "pick" us from a shelf that contains hundreds of others. So in order to understand why the color of our onionskin in this developmental model has such an effect on how and why people choose us, we must attempt to understand how the effects of race and gender play out on the overall development of racial identity development in the biracial community.

In order to do this, we must revisit the dark days in our nation's history that involve the impact of slavery, miscegenation and the history of the one-drop rule that continues to pervade even the most liberal and abstract minds of our times. For far too long, systems of state, education, criminal justice, politics, housing, medicine, and economics have been institutionalized to enforce racist ideology that began hundreds of years ago. While these systems affect blacks and Latinos to varying degrees based on the darkness and lightness of their skin color, mixed-race children and biracial individuals in total are caught in the middle.

105

On a daily basis, biracial people are forced to pick a side and find themselves having to self- identify based on whether they appear to look white or appear to look black, "referring to those physical traits that are typically associated with whites and those that are typically associated with blacks." [23] I can not tell you how many times I am asked to qualify something I have said or something I have done based on how other people perceive me and what I'm supposed to stand for based on the color of my skin.

Even though these situations cause me to feel frustrated, I try not to hold others responsible for their ignorance. By learning about this powerful need to judge I have been led to one of the historical places where these judgmental ideals originated. It is in this realm that I learned of how stratification within white and black societies became rooted in race and how a value was assigned to the color of skin.

In my experiences, no matter what level of understanding and comfort I came to have about my own racial identification, I found that others in my external environment would set traps for me and judge me based on my responses to their selfish and self-serving questions. At one time in my life, I exerted a pro-black, almost militant stance and began to embrace everything black while admonishing everything white. I found creative ways to dismiss my white mother and the rest of my white family when other black people would challenge my precepts or me.

As I became more aware of the black struggle, I also became aware of the benefits that were being enjoyed by other black people who had assumed more of a laissez-faire attitude when it came to the black struggle and all of its inherent controversies, limitations and setbacks. The power held within the color of my skin was becoming clearer to me as I initiated myself into testing the waters of relaxing my political stance and allowing myself to be accepted within the margins of white America. The more I allowed white people to experience me for the tanned appearance that I presented, the more I experienced being offered opportunities to be accepted and judged by white standards and protocol.

Throughout the majority of my life, I found myself going "black" and forth between the white and black margins of my external environment. Rather these two extremes kept finding me, all the while demanding that I live within the typeset margins that exist along the peripheral of their existence. In some hypersensitive way, I accepted living in the external fringes of my environment; my existence being based on the level of acceptance and understanding I would solicit from showing and sharing bigger and larger parts of me.

I can tell you one thing for sure. This game of back and forth played on a daily basis, if not a moment-to-moment basis, is exhausting. These types of interactions are emotionally draining and, in my opinion, exist to force biracial people to live inside of the comfort zones of white and black people.

Living inside of these predefined margins provides us with no real access to the full feast that sits in the banquet hall. Yet biracial people find themselves exerting superman-type levels of energy in order to be accepted by others on a daily basis. Needless to say, this process, this freak show of an existence, can leave you very, very spiritually and emotionally hungry for something real: a relationship, a connection, and sometimes, a way out.

There are always those instances, given our mental and emotional acuity, when we can trick ourselves into believing that the outside world is ready for us: to embrace us and love us and understand and accept a hundred percent of us over and

107

over again. However, having given in to this trickery time and time again, I do believe that we set ourselves up for failure as we continue to try to live in someone else's world. As a biracial woman and having struggled for most of my life to fit into the extremes of either the far right or the far left, I have come to the generous and freeing conclusion that I should spend more of my energies building up my own palace in my own world.

By becoming more and more comfortable with my unique traits and characteristics I define a life that resonates with my perception and my appearance. This is the palace in which I want to reside. It may have taken years but once my palace was built, I even became comfortable inviting the lefties and the righties over to get to know me: biracial Tiffany, on my terms and within my comfort level.

Fifteen

The Legacy of Race and the
Catch 22 of the "One Drop Rule"

During my coaching sessions, community workshops and group presentations many people ask how all of this racism stuff ever got started in the first place. I will now take a moment to try to explain, for those individuals who find themselves reading this book (and who may or may not already know), why it is important for everyone and anyone trying to understand the biracial experience to become familiar with the legacy of race. By understanding the historical legacy of race in our society, you become aware of the reasons for the racial stratification that continues to exist today.

By understanding the dynamics of racial stratification, you are forced to discuss the "one drop rule" that has so dramatically altered the landscape of individuals living in our society. The one drop rule does this by using the notion of race as a biological entity that pre-determines those of us "who have" and those of us "who have not" in our society. Historically, our great nation instituted the "one drop rule" that required any person with any drop of black in their ancestry, to self-identify as a black person. "Because the one-drop rule operated as an unquestioned assumption held by researchers, racial identity was not understood as a negotiable reality, nor was it an area where individuals had options."[24]

The innate nature of slavery created a system of racial stratification that chose to value people based on the color of their skin. Understanding the legacy and effect of the one-drop rule within our make up as individuals, families, and community means to understand the idea of privilege being assigned based on skin color and racial heritage. The racial group that was bestowed privileges was seen as having a higher value and therefore, never had to see race or understand how the idea of being devalued shaped the lives and realities of people of color. Unless the privileged racial class finds itself a minority in numbers, they do not have to accept, understand, see or feel how something as random as race can influence their choices or life experience on a daily basis. [25]

Based on the legacy of the one-drop rule, because my father is black, one would presume that I could only identify with and as a member of the black community. If this were the case, the joke would be on me because I didn't learn about my black heritage until my mid-twenties. Wait a minute. The joke *is* on me because this is what society expected of me even in the early 1990s.

No wonder I was so confused! Even today, given the "advances" seen since the end of the civil rights movement and the abolishment of Jim Crow laws, the effects of racial stratification between and amongst whites and blacks and between and amongst members of the black community continue to exist and affect how mixed-race individuals develop their racial identity.

Even though racial segregation was outlawed in the 1960s, the damage was already done.

Hundreds of years passed where we saw whites and blacks separated and divided. This same type of derisiveness existed between multicolored black and brown peoples throughout the land that became defined as the Americas. For far too long, light skinned black individuals received the benefit of appearing more favorable to the ruling white (European) class and the white elite (policy makers) inserted the foundational layers of what would become racial stratification into black communities.

From this "playing favorites" type of mentality arose a sense of hostility and a level of distrust between light and dark skinned blacks that had never existed before. Even today, examples of this deep chasm still exist within the black community and is evidenced by long held stereotypes and judgments all based on the varying degrees and concentrations of melatonin found in people's skin. While this type of racial stratification and segregation was felt and understood within communities, the creation of the national census saw the ushering in of a push toward the use and acceptance of racial classification "which categorized the population by occupation, religion, place of birth, citizenship, and race, among other characteristics." [26]

Today we continue to receive information with our morning cup of coffee that brings us up to date on the newest figures regarding the average life span, crime rates, divorce rates, numbers of individuals claiming unemployment and the number of teenage girls giving birth all over the world. "What's the big deal" you ask? These socio-economic figures are broken down by a single theme, angle, perspective and opinion: race.

The newsman or newswoman begins by telling us that these figures represent the national statistics and overall condition of our country. Then they proceed to inform us, almost convince us it seems at times, how these same statistics and figures are supposed to make us feel. Eduardo Bonilla-Silva states

> *"News reports on affirmative action seldom address the whiteness of academia or the workplace and its implications; sensational re-*

ports on welfare cheats never address the reality of welfare; that people on welfare live below the poverty line; stories of 'bad' behavior by black and Latino youths are presented as 'normal', whereas stories depicting 'bad' behavior by white youths are not. News reports on minorities thus tend to be presented as morality tales that support the various racial stories of the color-blind era. These reports are then recycled by the white audience as absolute truths ('Didn't you hear about the black guy who couldn't read and was admitted into Harvard? It was on the news.'). Therefore, the media uses the racial stories we create and makes them as if they were independent creations that validate our racial angst." [27]

What these very convincing news people politely refrain from telling us is whether any of these statistics and figures represent an actual mathematical number or whether they represent a statistical interpretation. "Why is *this* important?" you ask? The difference between whether the numbers represent a mathematical figure or statistical analyses is stark. Once you understand the difference between the two, you will realize why it is important that we, as a family, community and a society at large, should begin to understand how the figures can and do, play a key role in summarizing and understanding the racial identity development of our biracial children within a social context. [28]

In his book, Thicker Than Blood: How Racial Statistics Lie, Tukufu Zuberi explains and defines mathematics and statistical analyses:

"Mathematics is a system of statements that are accepted as true. Mathematical statements follow

one another in a definite order according to certain principles and are accompanied by proofs. The numbers from mathematics are the result of logical calculations. In mathematics the numbers are either exact or have a known or estimable error." [29]

He goes on to state,

"Statistics is a system of estimation based on uncertainty. Statistics is a form of applied mathematics. Often in statistics, the numbers are no more than the axioms applied and may have little to do with the conditions of the correct applicability in the real world." [30]

With the increase of the number of mixed-race individuals found around the globe, we find mixed-race individuals who are beginning to resist the protocol to self identify with narrowly defined boxes on census forms and other federal forms and applications that require some sort of racial self-identification. This challenge is nothing new to the thinkers and philosophers that have dotted our social and political landscape over the last two hundred years. W.E.B Du Bois was one of the first members of the African-American community to provide an evidenced-based challenge to the belief that racial differences were evolutionary in their creation. "Since the Enlightenment, conceptions of identity have defined the very core of questions about human difference in the Western world." [31]

As nations and peoples turned from communities with economies based in slavery, societies entered into a more modern age. While discussions and research into the transition of social science was oftentimes thwarted, there existed communities of intellectuals who began to look differently at the ways in which individuals began to consider a sense of self. The realities of race and ethnicity, and the complex racial stratifications that resulted, enabled people of all colors, shades and hues, to divide themselves on the sole basis of skin color.

While it is obvious that the power of the resultant classification systems continue to run deep even in today's modern world, during the seventeenth and eighteenth centuries, race and ethnicity were treated as second fiddle during times when people were focused on the division of peoples by class and wealth. W.E.B. Du Bois was one of a handful of people who believed that one could learn about the inherent qualities of the division of peoples by class and wealth only after understanding the racial stratification that was created with the introduction of slavery in the new worlds. [32] And so the conversation continued.

As political parties came and went, the relationships between whites and blacks were examined time and time again. These relationships were governed, clear policies were outlined and the individuals who had enough wealth, power and access to more of each to define class and social protocol enforced codes of conduct. So much attention was paid to the two racial extremes that the voice of the mixed race person became less distinct on the floors of government buildings and less a priority in the halls and conference rooms of educational institutions.

With all of the policy that was written into law around this same time, many researchers, teachers and political figures began to categorize mixed-race individuals as "confused" and in "denial." While these scholars prided themselves on their new and enlightened way of thinking about peoples of color, these same scholars and researchers tended to re-move any and all racial signifiers from their own conversation while they continued to be comfortable using words like "white" and "black". As the biracial population continued to grow and seek a voice in the community, areas of industry and education, the decision makers failed to properly rationalize and appropriately acknowledge the existence of the mixed race population. When they were directly approached by or dealt intimately with individuals who saw themselves as something more than white *or* black *and* more than white *and* black, these scholars couldn't resonate with a life experience that didn't fit within their prescribed boxes of interest and understanding.

Over time, (within the last twenty years) it became clear that there was a need for additional research to better understand the minds and lives of biracial people and the actual process of how mixed-race individuals develop their racial identity. Given the demographic of the multiracial population that continues to evolve and grow worldwide, people everywhere are becoming more acclimated to a racial climate that includes many different and exotic looking peoples from many different places.

Sixteen
History Lessons and New Perspectives

The history books that guided my educational process contained very little content about the color fabric of our country and our history. There was very little mention of historical peoples who today, in any of their given cultures, would be known or defined as a Mestizo, Mulatto or biracial peoples. The statistics and stories that I heard were always one of a white person saving the world.

The stories began with a description of a new island or country being discovered that was full of "little brown brothers" running wild, looking like savages and in need of a god that always appeared white. Whether it was the Boston Tea Party, the fight for independence or the heartache and brutality of the Civil War, people of color were often portrayed as a sidekick. History books made the practice and act of slavery seem like white, gun bearing men were doing black people a favor by removing them from the wild shores of the continent of Africa or the West Indies and giving them a life that would allow them to prosper and survive far better than their previous realities.

I was in the eighth or ninth grade before I ever heard that black people were responsible for many important discoveries and industries that ultimately affected our nation's ability to prosper. Until I attended a black history day service I had never met men and women whose families were two or three generations removed from slavery. I heard first hand accounts of the struggle that many dark skinned black people had undergone.

Even more eye opening was the struggles that many of the very light skinned (could pass for white) people were still experiencing. Within their communities, churches, and families light skinned blacks who could pass were experiencing horrors and prejudice that resonated deeply with me. While I heard and felt the experiences of these people whom I met, I still had no clue where this left me. I had no clue whether they were talking about me when they said white or when they said black. I felt I could be both but even then, I didn't think that being both was an option for me.

Recently, racial statistics have been used by social scientists in an attempt to refute arguments that were seen as racist and to "vindicate past misdeeds." [33] However, the actual use of these very same racial statistics may have, in hindsight, legitimized the use of methodologies that allow the problems they seek to overcome to continue to flourish. "Studies relying on assumptions that impose a decontextualized racial identity in a social stratum should be replaced by better studies that incorporate more accurate assumptions." [34]

It wasn't until the late 1980s and early 1990s that sociologists, educators and researchers opened the science field. Areas of developmental behavior, sociology, psychiatry and psychology saw new frameworks ushered in that reclassified mixed-race individuals. These attempts to understand the biracial life experience are the first of their kind and ultimately challenged the "one size fits all" [35] approach that was widely accepted and in circulation for all previous years.

The introduction of this newly minted research and data was actually collected by a number of mixed-race researchers and scholars who were new to the scene and the hallways of universities. These biracial individuals provided intellectually stimulating and unique perspectives on race, ethnicity, racial development and racial identification. These new beliefs, perspectives and models have just recently begun to profoundly affect and alter the way biracial individuals are perceived, understood, identified and accepted in our society today.

With the introduction of well-researched options, people are beginning to talk. They are communicating differently and building a comfort level that allows them to dialogue about what it is to be white, black and biracial today. People are changing their opinions and beliefs about how biracial individuals may actually be different than their all white or all black parents and peers.

People today are beginning to realize that biracial individuals can and do behave differently to stimuli in their environments. No longer are we expected to act black just because we have a little color in our skin. No longer are we seen as something so foreign when we are dark skinned and yet speak, dress and act in a way that was once reserved for our white counterparts.

In today's ever changing world, it is becoming more accepted that different ways and choices exist for people "of color" to become self-aware of their cultural heritage. We have choices when it comes to understanding our place in the world and ultimately, other people in the world have choices when meeting, playing, living and loving us. I happen to agree with this new ideology.

I believe that we can make well-informed choices and change our attitudes about long held cultural and racial ideals, only after becoming more informed, educated and experienced in how others learn and grow and understand themselves. And the more experiences the better! As a biracial individual, I understand that most of the time, people who don't know me are curious about me.

119

I understand that we make judgments and perceptions of one another based on the color of our skin, the texture of our hair and the style of our clothes. What I am hoping others understand after reading this book is that those judgments and perceptions don't have to be based on slavery, negative images or legacies. I want people to understand that it's ok to have judgments and preconceived notions after seeing someone and before meeting them.

It is ok to have these preconceived notions as long as you wait to form an opinion about the person until after you actually interact with them. Get a sense of how the person self-identifies. In this way, all effrontery can be put on hold and in its place, people, especially biracial individuals, will feel more comfortable to meet people with the self-identity that works best for them.

Whether you are meeting a biracial person for the first time or the thirtieth time, if the biracial person has chosen an identity in stark contrast to one that you are comfortable with, you can make a decision to accept it or not. Without judgment or fear you can choose to meet the biracial person in their realm of comfort. In this way you are allowing yourself to be accepted equally and as well.

If however, you choose to make the biracial person feel uncomfortable by challenging their chosen identity then I would suggest that your own racial identity development needs work. If you feel a need to point out and communicate (actively or passively) all of the reasons why you feel that the biracial people should not feel free to express themselves, then I suggest that you work on learning how to meet people where they are instead of where you need them to be. In this situation, it would be best if you were honest and expressed your level of discomfort right away before you end up saying or doing something that would cause you to look even more developmentally paused than you may actually be.

Having witnessed the gamut of these situations I admit that these situations are never easy. However, everyone: white, black and biracial, has the choice to educate themselves about one another and to make well-informed choices and decisions when it comes to our own knowledge and understanding of race relations. So let's talk about what it is to be biracial.

Seventeen
What it Means to Be Biracial

When someone expresses an opinion about being white, we all, all of us have the ability to understand something about "whiteness". Likewise, when someone expresses an opinion about being black, we all, all of us have the ability to understand something about "blackness". [36] What do you think of when you hear someone use the term "biracial"?

Do you get mixed ideas? Do you begin to picture famous celebrities or photos of beautiful babies with light colored skin and green eyes? Either way you put it, when people think of "biracial" there is no clear cut idea or thought that one has to represent what it is or what it means to be biracial or consisting of, made up of or derived from two or more races.

For the first time in history the question of race was given a makeover on the 2000 Census form. Most significantly, with the debut of the 2000 US Census, respondents were given the option of selecting one or more race categories to indicate racial identities. "Why is this important?" you ask, here's why: Until the debut of the 2000 US Census all people, no matter their total racial makeup, had to find and identify themselves within five preconceived racial and ethnic groups: American Indian or Alaska Native, Asian or Pacific Islander, Hispanic, non-Hispanic black, or non-Hispanic white. So for a biracial person like me who is not fully white and not fully black, we had to choose a side: fully white or fully black.

Well, if you are anything like me, I refused to live life within these narrow little boxes so I would select anything that applied. I was the person selecting both the white box and the black box when it came to choosing a racial categorization. I thought that by doing this, I was doing more than making a statement about race and identity.

I thought that somewhere "behind the scenes" someone was going to have to count me as something other than just white *and* black. What I didn't know, until recently in fact, is that even when this progressive type of categorization occurs, to many institutions, the individual that selects something other than white is still classified as black. In fact Princeton University admits the following,

> *"Until 2004, prospective students who checked more than one category on the application form were classified by the University according to their minority racial group-for example, a student who checked both black and white was considered by Princeton to be black. That changed with the admission of the Class of 2009: Since then all incoming students who select more than one race are classified as 'multiracial'. The classes of 2012 and 2013 each have 60-70 multiracial students-about 5.5 percent of each class."* [37]

With the recent release of the 2010 Census data we are able to see how biracial or mixed race people (individuals who identify themselves as consisting of two or more races) actually identified themselves when no one else was looking. Given the technical aspect of the information outlined within the actual Census 2010 data, I have provided a copy of the actual data for your review in Appendix A. If you, as did I, decided to choose both the white and black boxes, or the two or more races box and then described yourself as white *and* black, how can we be sure that the people "behind the scenes" have correctly categorized us at all?

In fact, unless we attend Princeton University, we cannot be sure how we will actually be counted. If we cannot be sure how we are actually counted, then how can we describe where we actually belong? Isn't being biracial all about identifying with some group that has an identifiable face? Is there really any freedom in our ability to choose a racial categorization if, no matter the racial identity developed, you are deemed black above all else?

What about this process seems fair to you? What part of racial categorization seems necessary and appropriate in our so called modern world? More importantly, in terms of the social issue, just where are biracial individuals or people born of mixed-race parents, supposed to fit in?

PART FIVE
Color Blind
A Mixed Girl's Perspective on Biracial Life

Eighteen
Racial Stratification and its Implications on Intraracial Relationships Today

So what does it mean to be something so different from the white and black (or whatever your racial heritage may be) people who created us? In order to get to the heart of this question, let's take another trip down history lane and let us consider the word "mulatto" which denotes the first generation offspring of a black and white individual. The word is Spanish in origin and predates the term biracial.

In Spanish, mulatto means hybrid. Mulatto existed as an official census category until 1930. In the Southern United States, mulattoes inherited slave status if their mothers were slaves. As for free mulattoes, in Spanish and French-influenced areas of the South prior to the Civil War (particularly New Orleans, Louisiana), a number of mulattoes were free and slave owning.

Although it is sometimes used to describe individuals of mixed European and African descent, it originally referred to anyone with mixed ethnicities. In fact, in the United States, "mulatto" was also used as a term for those who were of African American and Native American ancestry during the early census years. Mulatto was also used interchangeably with terms like "turk", leading to further ambiguity when referring to many North Africans and Middle Easterners. In addition, the term "mulatto" was also used to refer to the offspring of whites who intermarried with South Asian indentured servants brought over to the British American colonies by the East India Company.

For example, a Eurasian daughter born to a South Asian father and Irish mother in Maryland in

1680 was classified as a "mulatto" and sold into slavery. [38] Although still in use, in the last half century the term mulatto has fallen out of favor among some people and may be considered offensive by some in the United States. Today the preferred terms are generally biracial, multiracial, mixed-race and multiethnic.

Throughout the inter-mixing of different races that occurred in the early history of our country, many different colored children were born as blacks, whites and Native Americans married and mated. [39] In the early 1800s "a three-tiered social system evolved in the lower south, with mulattos serving as a buffer class between whites and blacks." [40] Living and loving during our early history revealed a unique awareness between individuals within the black community that focused on the value of skin color.

Having inherited characteristics that gave them the ability to pass for white, many biracial individuals sought to distance themselves from dark-skinned blacks. This is another reference to the racial stratification that exists within the black community even today. As a people, Americans are familiar with the principle that is written in our Declaration of Independence and which, theoretically, separates our culture from many other countries and places around the world: "all men are created equal." [41]

I am not sure what this phrase means to you but to me, while in school and reading this for the first time, I was perplexed. I was perplexed at the seemingly obvious meaning of this phrase and how the very nature of its meaning failed to truly factor into the immediate history and actions of the United States. How could a country appear on one hand to "get it" and with the other hand institute laws and provisions that almost guaranteed the devaluation of human life based solely on the color of a human's skin?

And it appears that I was not the only person to experience a sense of confusion after reading this phrase. The contradiction between the claim that "all men are created equal" and the existence of American slavery at the time of this phrase's utterance attracted comment even when the Declaration of Independence was first published. Congress, having made a few changes in wording, deleted nearly a fourth of the draft before publication, removing a passage critical of the slave trade, and many members of Congress, Jefferson included, owned black slaves during this same time.

In 1776, abolitionist Thomas Day, while responding to the hypocrisy in the Declaration, wrote:

> *"If there be an object truly ridiculous in nature, it is an American patriot, signing resolutions of independency with the one hand, and with the other brandishing a whip over his affrighted slaves." [42]*

Declaring the equality of all men did not prevent the United States from continuing the widespread practice of slavery, although abolitionists in anti-slavery arguments frequently raised the phrase. President Abraham Lincoln relied on the Declaration of Independence when making the case that slavery went against the deepest commitments of the American nation. Though he did so throughout the 1850s and into his presidency, the most famous example can be found in the Gettysburg Address:

> *"Four score and seven years ago our fathers brought forth on this continent a new nation,*

conceived in liberty and dedicated to the propo-
sition that all men are created equal."[43]

When Elizabeth Cady Stanton and others convened at the Seneca Falls Convention held in Seneca Falls, New York in July 1848, they drafted and signed a document titled the Declaration of Sentiments. The opening sentence alludes to this phrase:

> *"We hold these truths to be self-evident, that all men and women are created equal." [44]*

The phrase was also quoted by Martin Luther King, Jr. in his famous I Have a Dream speech, as the "creed" of the United States:

> *"I have a dream that one day this nation will rise up and live out the true meaning of its creed: 'We hold these truths to be self-evident: that all men are created equal." [45]*

Given the foundation on which our nation was built, and the ensuing movement for civil rights, many people today are under the impression that equal pay and opportunities exist for all people no matter the hue or color of their skin. The truth is that the United States remains a society defined and separated by race. Differences in definitions of success, opportunities, wealth, and failure are stark.

Per information documented in the 2002 U.S. Census and Fortune magazine, whites were found to have a higher percentage in the following categories than blacks: educational attainment, socioeconomic status and power. [46] In his book, Racism Without Racists, Eduardo Bonilla-Silva writes,

"Blacks and dark-skinned racial minorities lag well behind whites in virtually every area of social life; they are about three times more likely to be poor than whites, earn 40 percent less than whites, and have about a tenth of the net worth that whites have. They also receive an inferior education compared to whites, even when they attend integrated institutions. In terms of housing, black-owned units comparable to white-owned ones are valued at 35 percent less. Blacks and Latinos also have less access to the entire housing market because whites, through a variety of exclusionary practices by white realtors and homeowners, have been successful in effectively limiting their entrance into many neighborhoods. Blacks receive impolite treatment in stores, in restaurants, and in a host of other commercial transactions. Researchers have also documented that blacks pay more for goods such as cars and houses than do whites. Finally, black and dark-skinned Latinos are the targets of racial profiling by the police that, combined with the highly racialized criminal court system, guarantees their overrepresentation among those arrested, prosecuted, incarcerated, and if charged for a capital crime, executed." [47]

Most individuals don't look at all of these factors unless they are provided all at one time, usually in print, to be studied and dissected. If a person was presented a small piece of this information, one piece at a time, as spotted in our newspapers and discussed sparingly on the six o'clock news, the differences between whites and blacks would not seem to be so dramatic or apparent. When all of these small pieces come together and are studied in

133

their totality, the picture that is formed shows that most of us are living, learning, and praying within neighborhoods, schools and churches that look like us: meaning segregated and apart from members of our racially diverse counterparts.

Even after the end of the Civil Rights movement, many people continue to this day, to choose to live a life of segregation. Even among mixed-race populations, while dialogue continues about the vast differences that exist between whites and blacks, this dialogue remains a small percentage of the national conversation. America is beginning to change its attitude toward race.

It's kind of hard not to given the fact that America's population of multiracial people is rapidly increasing. In their book entitled, New Faces in a Changing America, authors Loretta I. Winters and Herman L. DeBose document the following statistics:

"In March 2001, the U.S. Bureau of the Census released race and ethnicity data showing that 2.4% of the population older than 18 years identified themselves as multiracial and, overwhelmingly, biracial (93%), but even more people younger than 18 years (4%) identified themselves as multiracial ('Poll,' 2001)." [48]

The statistics documented by the U.S. Census Bureau regarding children who are adopted and children who have a single parent or both parents who are racially different than the child show that there were less than 500,000 children in this category in 1960 compared with 1,937,496 in 1990. The U.S. Census Bureau also noted that there were 149,000 interracial marriages in 1960 compared with 964,000 in 1990 and 1,264,000 in 1997. [49]

In 2000, interracial marriages still only accounted for 2.9 percent of all marriages in the United States. And this figure represents only mixed-race marriages. While we are seeing growth in this diverse population (and not just due to the increased number of multiracial marriages and relationships) it begs the question; can people really believe or be under the impression that racism and prejudice really do *not* exist even when so many people are choosing to live separated from their racial opposite? "Because the ideology of white supremacy resides at the heart of most American institutions, it is virtually impossible to live in the United States and be immune to the numerous ways that notions of white supremacy are reflected in the attitudes and practices that shape our society." [50]

There are times when I find myself visiting clients, friends and yes, sometimes even family members. I'm not sure if its because they know me and feel comfortable with me or because they don't associate a lot of my mannerisms with the "typical" black person, but these individuals will make comments about other races and then say to me that they feel comfortable saying this because, "well, you understand and we know we can say these things to you". This is happening in white homes and black homes and to each, it is obvious to me that I don't represent enough of the other to prevent them from saying something derogatory or negative about their racial opposite.

I can tell you that nothing else reflects my being biracial more than these experiences. And I bet you are thinking that I only hear whites talking about blacks and vice versa? Well if you said this or believed this then you would be wrong.

The amount of racial or prejudicial comments I hear coming from black people toward other black people is just as high as comments made by white people toward black people and by black people toward white people. In fact, while beginning to navigate the world of white versus black and black versus white, I came upon this interesting, appalling and even more frustrating world of black on black judgment and oppression. Many people that I speak with believe that no one person or thing can come between the feeling and sentiment of black fraternity or brotherhood. Well I disagree and I disagree strongly.

Many people believe that black solidarity is impenetrable, that intra racial color discrimination is a thing of the past. To understand the possible harmful effects of color blindness, one would have to become aware of the existence of the racial stratification that exists among and within the black community. "Traditionally, the color complex involved light-skinned blacks' rejection of blacks who were darker. Increasingly, however, the color complex shows up in the form of dark-skinned African Americans spurning their lighter-skinned brothers and sisters for not being black enough." [51]

Color consciousness within the black community affected everyone: masters, servants, slaves and lovers. The power of color and a systematic valuation of color became evident between blacks that were classified as dark-skinned and light-skinned, mulattos, Creoles and Native Americans. This system became almost as strong a racial classification system as the one that existed between whites and blacks. [52]

From this racial awareness came a desire by many within their own communities to separate from the masses. Many of the individuals who were mixed or Creole wanted to be seen and heard as something entirely different than their dark-skinned counterparts. No matter their desire, the existence of the one-drop rule, focusing on any black racial heritage in their bloodline, continued to recognize the lack of pure whiteness within these individuals.

As evidenced by our anxiety over discussing race relations today, there remains a lack of understanding by whites and blacks when it comes to the biracial experience. "The elitism that had begun before the Civil War became further entrenched after it, and still remains evident today in the color gap in power and privilege that divides the black community." [53] To further illustrate the isolation, whether by desire or decree, within the biracial communities after the Civil War, consider the number of social clubs that came to exist.

These clubs celebrated and operated solely on the basis of skin color and class. Take for instance the Bon Ton Society of Washington D.C. and the Blue Vein Society of Nashville. [54] Both were created to maintain bloodlines and a feel for the three tiered society reminiscent of the time when mulattos or biracial individuals felt that they benefited from an advantage of "serving as a buffer class between whites and blacks." [55]

Issues of class and race still exist within the black community. They appear to stem from the fact that, historically, the lightest-skinned members of minority communities were granted the highest amount of freedoms. These freedoms have provided better access to higher education and opportunities in careers. All of which have systematically been denied to their darker-skinned brothers and sisters. [56]

From these historical examples, it is easy to see that issues continue to exist between light-skinned and dark-skinned members of the black community. It is apparent that biracial children, their parents and extended family members can feel overwhelmed when trying to decipher the meanings and messages that exist within their own communities. Especially when it comes to a general response about color and race.

Given this presumed hardship, let us consider the plight of the biracial child when left alone, without resources, an outlet or access to a person of color. Without this assistance they have no way to deal with and navigate society at large. Not only do biracial children have to learn to navigate the racial and class pathway as created and moderated by whites but they have to learn the nuances that go along with living and learning cultural identity and legacies from and within the black community too.

Nineteen
The Fight Between Physical Appearances,
The Beauty Standard and Self Identity

When we look at how the physical traits and characteristics of mixed-race children are perceived, evaluated and responded to by the layers of our racial development onion, we have a tendency to assume that the majority of watchers and responders are white. While this may be true given the racial breakdown percentage of our population, I call your attention to the historical perceptions and associated meanings of the black intraracial community. Just as important among blacks as whites is the concern for and perceptions of skin color, visibility of veins, hair texture, facial bone and nose structure and the color of one's eyes.

In the same way that these characteristics have been used by white society to identify, isolate and devalue blacks or mixed-race individuals, so too do the instances exist wherein black people and people of color base an idea of value and worth on these same external and very physical characteristics. There is, however, one example when the basis for the opinion stated above can be thrown out of the window.

Consider the experience that you have had with the "exceptional black" person in your life. Whether this person is black or biracial, a Hollywood media darling or an athletic star, the "exceptional person of color" defies all preconceived notions of race. Stereotypes and judgments reserved for unexceptional members of the black or colored class magically disappear.

When some level of fame or specialness is achieved, whites and blacks alike find some way to rationalize away all of the ideas and opinions they once held. When relegating a place in their lives for their new special friend, they will find a way to work with this new sense of blackness. No matter what this exceptional friend may look like or the values they may hold, all of the faults and characteristics that once defined them or limited their opportunities, seem to fall away while the number of people in their lives and in their external fringes try to claim them as one of their own.

Having already discussed the effect of physical appearance on the development of racial identity among mixed-race children, let us now consider how whites and blacks define beauty. Given how different mixed-race children appear from their all white or all black peers and counterparts, consider how the translation of the beauty standard is transferred to the struggles that mixed-race girls encounter during their racial identity development. It can be said that historically, most cultures are held to a standard of beauty that is more European than anything else.

With increasingly more parts of their self esteem being tied into appearance, mixed-race girls are even more susceptible to the European beauty standard because the physical attributes they have inherited appear to mirror the standard that was previously set. "Within the patriarchal paradigm that evaluates femaleness in terms of physical beauty based on whiteness/lightness, this affords an advantage to this subgroup of mixed-race girls and creates the tension that often exists between black mixed-race girls." [57] Black individuals, unless they have a parent that is racially different, will in most cases identify racially as black.

Whether light-skinned or dark-skinned, and no matter the social context in which they encountered many of their foundational experiences in life and love, they will identify themselves as black. However, given these same matters of life and love, a mixed-race individual may not always identify as all white or all black all of the time. And why should they?

Depending on the hue or shade of their skin, the color of the parent that was present most often, and access to cultural knowledge and resources, a mixed race individual should have the freedom to choose a racial identity that best reflects the cultural and personal identity that fits them best. Mixed race individuals should be free to self-identify as white, black or biracial given their encounters with people who accept or challenge their racial self-identity. They will choose any one of these racial identities based on how the degree and level to which their physical appearance is either accepted or rejected by both whites and blacks.

In most cases, the interactions with individuals who self-identify as only black have the potential to be negative for mixed-race individuals especially when these other black individuals assume that our desire to identify as biracial is a turning away of what it means to "be black". "With the ability to choose one's racial identity comes the possibility of rejection, real or perceived. There is an interactive cycle that occurs such that the more black girls sense mixed-race girls pulling away from their blackness, the more likely they are to reject them.

In turn, the more rejection mixed-race girls perceive, the more likely they are to pull away from blackness-and the cycle persists. At the heart of this pattern is perceived rejection from both sides and a great deal of pain for both parties." [58] And we have not even begun to discuss how the presence and attention of young men play into any one part of this complex racial development onion that we have created.

The color complex that we previously discussed stretches its ugly hand into the relationship between mixed-race girls and black girls who identify solely as black, especially when boys are factored into the acceptance equation. Remember, in family situations where the historical legacies of color and racial value have not yet been discussed, our society leans toward an acceptance of favoritism and privilege that is granted to lighter-skinned individuals. Working off of this premise, one can understand how dark-skinned individuals could feel devalued when compared to the standard of beauty that is normally accepted within our communities.

In fact, one only has to view our print and screen media to see the trend that glorifies lighter skinned individuals. If one were to believe or buy into the racial ideology as demonstrated in this media form, we can presume that there is a penchant (again speaking only for those individuals whose families fail to discuss the legacy of race relations) for men of color to respond, if not prefer, lighter-skinned individuals. If we are to believe what we see in media then this desire for lighter skin occurs even before darker-skinned individuals are given a chance to express their unique characteristics. What we fail to realize is that had darker skinned individuals been given the opportunity to express themselves to their potential suitors it may in fact reveal an individual who is more aligned with their own life experiences.

Needless to say, when the attention and presence of young men are added to the obstacles that young, mixed-race girls face while trying to form and accept their own racial identity, one could understand how feelings of resentment, anger, competition, rejection and distrust can be expressed between mixed-race girls and black girls who are not of a mixed racial heritage or background. If these feelings are experienced at an early enough age and during emotional and psychological development, mixed-race individuals could eventually end up generalizing the negativity that they experienced during the "competitions" they endured with black girls. Biracial girls could fall prey to accepting and expecting similar thought and behavior patterns from all black people they encounter throughout the rest of their lives.

The capacity for these negative experiences to permanently affect the emotional development of mixed-race individuals is considered an example of how the forces of several factors has historically invaded the way people of color come to understand themselves, in relation to other people of color and in relation to whites. The legacy of slavery, the adoption of the one-drop rule within the American psyche and the value of color and race that was inserted into the racial stratification in the black communities and within the white/black communities has shown a power like no other. This power causes mixed-race individuals especially, to internalize and develop a "racialized and gendered self-concept" [59] that causes people to relate and behave in certain negative ways with one another. "For hundreds of years, the forces of white supremacy and patriarchy have gnawed on the psyches of women and black people and, as a result, many have internalized negative messages about themselves and developed ways of relating with each other that reflect the attitudes and behaviors of whites and men as a collective." [60]

Twenty

Lessons to Learn- Not White Enough for White People and
Not Black Enough for Black People

For white parents raising biracial children, the idea of being able to prepare your child for the number of obstacles facing your family, even before considering the intraracial history, issues and relationships, can at times appear alarming and feel overwhelming. However, to fully understand the obstacles and issues facing your biracial child, you must have an understanding and awareness of the cultural and historical issues that exist within all or both of your child's racial heritages. "Ignorance of another's culture only breeds racism." [61]

Parents need to become educated about all of the ways that messages of devaluation bombard our biracial children on a daily basis. Parents and children need to become comfortable learning and communicating together in order to create strategies with which to combat these messages. It would be difficult for any one person or family unit to develop positive strategies and defend against racist or stereotypical messages that could become internalized.

For the parents and families raising children of color, life can become especially difficult if you do not garner support from significant allies and role models. You must become comfortable accessing people who are capable of consciously recognizing negative messages. For the sake of your child, you must proactively insert balancing, positive images and messages of black culture into your life in an attempt to counteract the possible limiting effects on your child's overall and ultimate racial identity.

Children must be empowered and educated by caring individuals who value and understand race and skin color. Without access to these types of individuals biracial children run the risk of repeating a lifetime of experiences that are created from feelings of fear, isolation, powerlessness and anger. It should be understood that the possibilities outlined in this text are presumed to address the experiences of some, not all, of the biracial children that make up our global population.

Some of the experiences, feelings and development issues that can arise will affect biracial children whose parents are white, black, Asian, Latino, European, and Polynesian. This text does not assume that biracial children are only born to white and black parents. Most of the descriptions used in this text to demonstrate behaviors, trends or experiences are described using case scenarios of white, black and mulatto because that has been my life experience.

When describing instances of rejection, experiences can deal with feelings that can be implied to represent mixed-race children rejecting all of the following individuals: darker skinned blacks, lighter skinned blacks, and whites. Their expressions can also refer to any number of light skinned mixed- race individuals rejecting any number of their darker skinned Asian, Latino or Polynesian counterparts as well.

In his book, The Color of Water: A Black Man's Tribute to his white Mother, James McBride states,

> *"Being mixed is like that tingling feeling you have in your nose just before you sneeze-you're waiting for it to happen but it never does. Given my black face and upbringing it was easy for me to flee into the anonymity of blackness, yet I felt frustrated to live in a world that considers*

the color of your face an immediate political statement whether you like it or not." [62]

As a biracial individual I experienced almost every event in my life completely aware of the race of the individuals with whom I was interacting. In fact, both whites and blacks affected all of my life experiences. I had little to no interaction with other biracial individuals.

Without having anyone in my life that looked like me or someone who could have helped me navigate my feelings and experiences, I became a person that remained afraid for a very long time of truly experiencing or giving in to the emotions that I had when interacting with others. I was constantly wondering what people thought of me and how they expected me to behave. To explain the tightrope of confusion and angst that I was constantly walking I give you the following:

Imagine how confusing it would be to have two very different people: one black and one white, staring at you, questioning you and devaluing everything you have come to know and love about yourself. As that biracial child I wasn't sure if I was special or in trouble. While one would compliment me on my pretty green eyes and my grade of "good" hair, the other also told me that my kind wasn't allowed.

Can you guess which person said what? You'd be shocked to know that the white person was complimentary while the black person admonished me. This specific admonishment came when I was the only light-skinned girl in the bunch.

I was trying to get access to a darker skinned friend's roller skating party. Only later would I learn, as the others tried to explain, that had I been allowed to enter, I would have made all the other dark-skinned girls feels uncomfortable. My friend's parent who had issued the warning didn't want anything to spoil her little girls' special day. And so as shown in this example, I would continue on in my life, experiencing the mixed messages of black society.

Even later in my early adult life I would continue to be leery of some black people. I was confused and left wondering why, after accomplishing something good or becoming well known for a special achievement, black people who once isolated me, wanted to embrace me. I never considered that I could fit the role of a "unique black" person in someone else's life. Given the confusion I experienced on a daily basis regarding the meaning of the color of my skin, I certainly did not expect this reception from people within my own community.

I never imagined that people, after not wanting me or claiming me for so long, would all of a sudden want to lay claim to me and use me to satisfy some piece of their purpose. But they tried. And they did.

All of a sudden, a part of my world opened up and here I had whites and blacks pointing out the color of my skin or the distinct features of my face that screamed mixed-race heritage. And they pounced and tried to find a way that I could benefit them.

To be held at such an emotional precipice, with access fully into "their" world only when the feeling moved "them", had the potential to shake any preconceived racial identity with which I may have ever been comfortable.

I remember a time during my years at boarding school when the issues of race finally confronted my best friends and me. After many conversations about the colleges and universities that we wanted to attend, we had decided on the college trips that we would take individually and as a group. Given the fact that our boarding school was a college preparatory school, I knew the importance that was placed

148

on achieving a higher education. What I didn't realize was how much race played a factor in my friends choosing schools and more importantly, in the schools choosing my friends.

Boarding School had been a major transition in my life, albeit an easy one. The friendships that I made were solid and had opened my eyes to the ideas of ongoing relationships and cultural acceptance that spanned the entire globe. So the idea of making another transition into college, while I understood it was a necessary step in my overall evolution, did not excite me as it appeared to ignite a fire in my friends.

Wanting to remain a deep part of their lives, I quietly dived into the daily highs and lows of preparing for our college trips that appeared to define my friends' existence. I listened to their deep conversations as they planned the road trip that would allow them to experience the most campuses over a certain number of days. I received an expedited history lesson on the significance of historically black colleges and universities and even learned a few new dance moves in the event we were called to perform if we were lucky enough to be invited to any of the off campus parties while visiting these chosen schools in the south.

While watching my friends prepare for our road trip, I was taken in with the sense of confidence and surety each one of them displayed. They had been able to choose a school in their desired location and stay true to the historical and cultural legacies they were familiar with. At the same time, they remained excited about a transition that would take us all into an unknown that was very different from the sheltered lives we were experiencing while living on campus at boarding school.

I would be lying if I said that I wasn't excited about spending twelve hours in a car with my two best friends. Prior to boarding school I had traveled very little and had never really tested the boundaries of our very small and isolated town located off the northeastern coast of Lake Erie. Needless to say, I couldn't wait to load up the car, get on the road, listen to our mix tapes and share all of the details of the trysts and turns of our romantic lives (and yes girls attending an all girls boarding school do have romantic lives with boys at other schools!).

My friends decided it was time that I learn about the culture of an all girl, all black school. Eager to show me the very reasons they were so excited for the next chapter in their lives, they made sure that we spent the next couple of Saturday nights watching movies that featured cameo appearances by Spike Lee and Kid & Play. Imagine this: small time mixed girl forced to watch mean spirited interactions between black female characters who were fighting one another all because this girl's hair was straight or this other girl who was very, very light skinned was being flirty with a guy whose girlfriend was darker skinned.

Here it was all over again: racism, prejudice and hate on video and being celebrated by girls who I thought were my best friends. Were they serious? Did they actually think that I would want to A) attend these types of colleges knowing the racial issues that seemed to exist in every single facet of daily life and B) think I was going to drive down to Georgia and walk into an atmosphere where my skin color could possibly be blamed for whether or not they got into their chosen school?

The image of light skinned girls constantly fighting with their darker skinned counterparts was not appealing to me. I could not imagine how I would go

150

about trying to prove any sort of racial claim to any certain race given the fact I could not even have a conversation with my mother about the real identity of my father, let alone his color, race or nationality. Needless to say fear took hold of me.

I began waking up from dreams that found me stepping into a college auditorium for scheduled meet and greets. In this chaotic and estrogen filled environment I was bombarded by college admission representatives and leaders of clubs and cliques who were begging me for my vote of confidence while asking me to sign on the dotted line. In these harrowing dreams I saw myself running and trying to keep up with my darker skinned girlfriends who were themselves running to keep up with the college professors and admission board members.

In these dreams my dark skinned girl friends could not get a moment of time to speak to the important people in order to relay their desire and passion to gain entry into these schools. I too was powerless to escape the crowd that was vying for my attention. I tried not to offend anyone while running this way and that way constantly looking for a way out of all of the color that seemed to surround my lightness and naïveté.

How could I ever tell my two best friends that their movies scared the hell out me? What were the words that I should have used to inform them that the part of "black life" they had introduced me to was not something that I ever wanted to experience if I could ever help it? Did this realization on my part signify a fear of black people that may have had a deeper meaning than even I was prepared to admit?

In response to this nightmare I did what came naturally. I began to come up with excuses that would keep me on campus and apart from the road trip that we had been preparing for over the last couple of weeks and months. It hurt me to see my girlfriends drive off without me and I knew that when they returned, many, many things were going to be different.

While I thought I was doing us all a favor, I could not have been any more unprepared for what happened when they returned. My darker skinned friends had been transformed. All that I had been with them and for them no longer existed and I was again banished to the margins of biracial life.

To my racially confused mind I saw their stares and glances land on the color of my skin. When the meaning of their response finally sunk in, I was hurt beyond belief to know that our friendships could be over just like that. I began to receive cold receptions and became the butt of many of their jokes. I felt the sting of inherited prejudice and it hurt.

This wasn't the first time but it was the most memorable time in my life when the sting of words spoken by my black friends hit deep and made me even more aware of the color of my own skin, the texture of my hair and the color of my eyes. Whether it was the interaction that I missed out on over two twelve hour rides or the sharing of the college experience, I will never know. What I do know is that my two darker skinned friends gave up all appearances of formality and began to question me as if we had never shared secrets in the middle of the night or played in the same basketball games as outstanding members of the same team.

I continued to hope that time and space would allow us to move past this hiccup and we would get back to living on campus together and that things would be just like they had been before. Never would I have imagined that my two best friends would return to boarding school from their trip to an all black, all girls school and assault the motive of my skin color with their unspoken questions and unformed words; once and for all ending the closeness that we all had once shared. In fact, while the college trip to Georgia affected me in ways that would eventually alter how I chose friends in the future, it didn't prove to be the first.

I remember very early on in my life of being aware of the potential of rejection based on my light colored skin and my "good" hair. It always seemed that if I took two steps forward in the white community, rejection by a person or a challenge of anything that I came to know as something "Tiffany", forced me to retreat ten steps in the opposite direction. In response to this constant rejection by whites I would run to the black community (even against my mother's covert wishes).

I would seek out reassurance or encouragement from people I knew, thought I knew and yes, even complete strangers. Sometimes I received what little they were willing to give to the confused mixed girl from down the street but most of the time, I was shot down here too. The constant back and forth between racial opposites and cultural foes resulted in a lifetime of issues that I only recently have begun to understand. While researching texts and materials for this book, I have, for the first time in my life, found the vocabulary to talk about my racial identity, my life experiences and my overall development of self that couldn't have come from anything other than the life experiences that I present to you today.

Twenty-One
Pushback- Why "Being" Biracial Isn't Really a Choice

What I couldn't have known then, while enduring racism and prejudices from both whites and blacks, children and adults, girls and boys, was that there would be so many other biracial individuals who needed to see and hear someone with my history and my story. Speaking out about the things that happened in my life places me in a unique position that enables me to relate to and help others deal with similar characteristics and experiences. While my early biracial life was filled with confusion, hatred, misunderstanding and chaos I know that God had a plan the entire time.

God has granted me insight and has provided me with all of the tools to pull all of my experiences together. Whether you are reading this book and are the parents, caregivers, friends, family members or educators raising or impacting the lives of biracial people, we can help one another. We can relate to one another's experiences and challenges and we can share what we have learned with others in order to prevent any further confusion and hate from trickling downward and outward into someone else's life. We can relate to one another whether we are women in a biracial relationship; biracial children trying to communicate with our parents and peers; or parents and extended family members seeking to understand and become more educated on the issues faced by our biracial children.

God has always had a purpose for me. In His own way, he has allowed my unique life experience to embody a diverse and challenging story. While there were times that I felt a lack of guidance and assistance, He has allowed me to tap into what has always been there: a quiet and consistent sense of knowing that something greater existed.

By tapping into the very source that gave me life, I am learning to manifest all of the fruits that He created just for me when he allowed my essence to be born into this world. Through this faith defying relationship I am learning to love myself. I am getting to know, understand and trust the truly divine presence that exists within me that allows me to give all that I have and all that I am to others.

Only in this way and with this life experience can I give the highest thanks to God. By accepting the parents that He gave me, by enduring the treatment and the disgust of the people who turned away from me, and honoring every individual He has brought into my life to love me: He has saved me. All of these experiences, all of these people, all of this time has allowed me to understand that the greatest form of "thank you" is giving all that I am to all of the individuals who need a little or a lot of anything that I have to give.

Like some biracial children today, my black father was never in the realm of my life consciously, emotionally or physically before I saw the age of thirty. I say this to remind you that during my formative years I never had an opportunity to learn about my blackness from a culturally relevant person, let alone a family member. While I do not remember my mother ever specifically saying or commanding me to not hang out with black kids, I do remember my mother never being quite happy (as happy as she was when I was with white kids) when I was playing outside, playing dress up or getting my hair done by black girls.

I have two vivid memories. One captures my mother hugging me and smiling-almost gushing- as I danced around our living room, singing along to

Nancy Sinatra's entire <u>These Boots are Made for Walking</u> album while I swayed and danced with a long towel on my head, secured by a plastic claw like clip. I felt special, just like the long haired, white entertainer I was emulating.

Contrast this image to the one where my mother's voice breaks through the blaring music screaming out from the boom box radio that was playing Janet Jackson's song, "Control". My girlfriends and I, one black and one Puerto Rican, were in the field behind our apartment, dancing and mimicking Janet's moves. Seeing me like this, my mother responded with threats of violence and commanded me to get in the house before the neighbors see me acting like a slut.

Again, my mother never told me that white was right and black was bad but I began to feel like this could be the case. Based on my mother's two extreme reactions I noticed that the only difference that existed between the two women I was emulating was that one was black and one was white. Understanding the way my mother (and other white mothers I have come to know who are raising biracial children) responded to the instances in which she interpreted my actions and behavior as representing either a white or black action or characteristic, shows how important it is to understand the idea of context when examining the life of a biracial child.

Individuals who identify as biracial tend to experience the same types of cultural frameworks and social experiences across the board. As was my biracial life experience, when I removed the existence of a single parent of color, I found myself being raised and educated in environments that were predominantly white. I was one of a handful of students of color in every school that I attended and on a daily basis I shared in the same types of patterns and be-

157

haviors as my white peers when it came to tastes for food, fashion and fun.

Most biracial individuals fitting into this scenario end up identifying with a white racial identity. For both the biracial individual and their white peers, there are more similarities than differences. White peers reject that anything their biracial friend says or does is in any way related to the media portrayals of what it is to be and act "black".

Similarly, the biracial individual, using their own racial identity as a measuring stick, agrees with the assessment offered by their white peers and feels isolated and different than the media portrayal of what it is to be and act "black". "The mixed-race person fails to fit into either cognitive category "black" or "white" so both parties tacitly agree to a new identity-"biracial"- where biracial means, for both, something between black and white." [63] From this example one would believe that it is easy for both black and white individuals to accept the biracial identity as a legitimately valued option for mixed-race children.

The fact that black and white individuals have the power to influence the decision for a mixed-race child to want to self-identify as biracial is a problem in and of itself. Does it seem fair that we have created an environment in which a child assumes an identity that can be challenged, accepted or outright rejected by others? On one hand it is important to demonstrate how this type of situation forces biracial children to learn about the cultural and historical legacy of the one-drop rule. On the other hand we see the challenge that is created given the process that exists when others categorize them based on race and its assumed class and value.

Biracial children learn to adopt interaction skills by pushing back against the very individuals, organizations and institutions that try to put them into a box. While the outcome of this process can be positive and healthy, navigating the process of the push back and challenging the ideals and responses of loved ones can begin to play with a child's psyche. If the push back and challenge is thwarted or turns out to become a negative experience for the child, the only option that exists for the child is to reconsider the adopted racial identity, assess the emotional context and subsequent damage and try to develop another identity that resonates with their surroundings and other external factors.

Nothing about this option speaks to the biracial child responding to a clear sense of self. In fact, I challenge the validity of any new or edited version of racial identity that emerges from this type of process. "Those who understand themselves as biracial, but fail to have their self-understanding validated by others are trapped in the gray area between the one-drop rule and the multiracial movement, both of which have worked to define their racial identities in opposing directions." [64]

Today, many biracial and multiracial individuals who could "pass" for white choose to institute a reality where race does not play a part in their daily life or consciousness. These individuals have this choice because their physical characteristics and overall phenotype grants them membership into a group of privileged individuals. These people usually are the ones claiming that "people are just people," that they "don't see" race, and that they have "transcended race" altogether. [65]

Refusing to accept any racial identity at all can be indicative of a racial identity development that is considered to be healthy or unhealthy. It begs the question; if biracial individuals have a hard enough time being accepted and categorized for the unique characteristics that they inherit and develop from both whites and blacks, how much harder is it going to be for mixed-race individuals to obtain understanding and acceptance from society when they try to gain acceptance based on characteristics of their authentic self? Instead of relating with others based on ancestry, heritage and a common understanding, transcendent biracial individuals are asking to be accepted and understood based on whether they are a good person, play an instrument or speak another language.

I do believe that this is an ideal goal that we should strive for as we insert ourselves as individuals into the lives of family, friends and organizations. But before this type of personalized interaction can be allowed to take place, we must meet the front lines of classification head on. It is upon our first glimpse of one another that we take in a personalized meaning and assumption of a person's color and its ultimate value in regard to our knowledge of historical legacies.

When judging on the basis of color and having the nerve to ask others, "What are you?" we don't care about whether this person speaks twelve different languages, likes football or considers themselves to be good wives or husbands. What we are asking for is an immediate way to relate to others based on the way we have categorized others far too often in the past: on the basis of color and race. Whether we, as biracial individuals, find ourselves shopping for clothes, hailing a cab, entering a business establishment or walking in a neighborhood, we are seen and judged by others based on the color of our skin and the assumed race, behaviors and mentalities that are subsequently assigned to that color.

The frequency and quality of this judgment and assessment differs based on the darkness and lightness of skin tones and features found in our faces and hair textures. The acceptance or rejection of our chosen and expressed racial identity is evident as seen on the faces and in the words of the individuals we meet on a daily basis. As biracial individuals, we are either accepted or rejected based on the ability of others to develop their own level of racial under-standing, awareness and development.

PART SIX

Color Blind

A Mixed Girl's Perspective on Biracial Life

Twenty-Two
Racial Socialization- The Factors that Should Give Us Pause

There are many different ways in which multiracial children learn about race and racial values, norms and prejudices. Likewise, there are several ways that parents can experience and influence the way their children learn about the meaning, importance, and value of race in our society. In their book, <u>Raising Biracial Children</u>, authors Kerry Ann Rockquemore and Tracey Laszloffy describe how experiences surrounding race as experienced by parents: the type, duration, and extent of the relationship between parents and the way in which parents respond to the physical traits and characteristics of their children- all have an effect on how biracial children learn racial norms, meanings and social values. [66]

In my experience while all of these interactions involve some type of racial socialization and are quite important, physical appearance and the expression of physical traits seems to be the most divisive of the group. Physical traits and characteristics are the first things the public sees. Even before someone can form an opinion about the way words are spoken or ideals are expressed, judgments can be, and are, formed about the way a person looks.

Based on people's preconceived notions, pre-existing stereotypes and their understanding of racial valuation, mixed race children are, in my opinion, more subject to be defined and judged. The typecast is pre-set on the grade of their hair, the broadness of their nose, the color of their eyes and the hue of their skin tone. While reactions from the external world to a family's biracial child is also an important factor in the child's development of a racial identity, it is the response of the child's parents that remains the most important overall factor.

Consider the situation where a family is raising two mixed-race children. One child is fair skinned with "good" hair and light eyes. The other sibling is darker skinned with dark eyes and tight, curly hair. Since the immediate family members, specifically the mother and father, impact the children's sense of self to a higher degree than extended family members, the way the parents react to, respond to and encourage each child plays a significant role in each child's development of one another and of themselves. [67]

For any obvious and outward favoritism to be displayed by either parent, it would be considered unconscionable. Well what about the instances when either or both parents don't even realize that they are rewarding one sibling over another based on either parent's personal experiences or preconceived notions of race? When parents unconsciously reinforce stereotypes via covert actions and reinforcements, or ideals and behaviors learned during their very own racial identity development, they are unable to correct behaviors that were molded and embedded in many of their own early life experiences.

Interactions with immediate family members and parents can hinder, suppress or alter a biracial child's racial identity development. Perceptions, comments and stereotypes (made or expressed) by outside factors can wreak havoc on a biracial child's sense of self. Their overall understanding of race and racism within social, familial and societal relationships can be altered by something as simple as someone's slip of the tongue.

The confusion and havoc is felt first and foremost by the child but can also lead to feelings of frustration, depression and anger on behalf of the child's parents and family members. The degree to which outside factors can affect biracial children and the families and parents that love them depends on the amount of experience and frequency with which they encounter situations of public misperception and prejudice. Using the information contained within the pages of this text, I am asking and urging biracial individuals and the families raising mixed-race children to consider race differently.

Historically, race was defined as:

1. A local geographic or global human population distinguished as a more or less distinct group by genetically transmitted physical characteristics
2. A group of people united or classified together on the basis of common history, nationality, or geographic distribution: *the German race*
3. A genealogical line; a lineage
4. Humans considered as a group

The basis for these definitions is mostly biological, based on genetic characteristics as blood groups and metabolic processes. The foundations for these definitions continue to crumble as new information is gleamed from the human genome project and by the ever-increasing studies of multiracial life experiences around the world. "In other words, race is real insofar as people believe it is real, and that it has real consequences for people's life chances and opportunities." [68]

It is important to know that as parents, you have options and resources. You have help when it comes to preparing a strategy that can help to identify, assess and intervene with situations that can arise on behalf of your child as they navigate school or any similar setting that has the potential to affect the development of their racial identity. Parents can create an open and comfortable setting in which conversations about race or race relations are encouraged and discussed.

By feeling comfortable discussing race in the confines of home, mixed-race children learn to express issues with race or matters concerning race relations in a larger context and with varying groups of people and places. Parents are also encouraged to find out as much as they can about the school or learning environment in which their child spends time on a daily basis. By establishing a presence within the school environment and entering into a positive, encouraging relationship with school educators, parents place themselves into the framework of the institution and become a part of the solution as seen through the eyes of their children. Besides setting a positive image for the children, parents establish a solid foundation of trust and understanding with teachers prior to any one situation that would normally require parent-teacher interaction.

When we make ourselves available to find the truth in all situations, we open ourselves to experience freedom in its truest forms: Freedom of Expression, Freedom of Speech, Freedom of Thought, Freedom to Love and Freedom to Live. For me, during my formative years, as a biracial child, experiencing truth would have afforded me the opportunity to experience a sense of freedom wearing my hair in whatever form or fashion that would have made me happy to look in the mirror. I would have been free to say how I felt when I felt it without having to carry the burden of constantly trying to cushion the impact of my words, thoughts or feelings.

I would have been free to think of myself as the caring, non-judgmental, affectionate person that I felt I could be. If I had known my truth, the fear of expressing these characteristics with others would have been removed. I would have been free to express my love and affection toward white men and black men (even if they were just boys at this age) in a way that would have allowed me to show and share my innocence, my naïveté and my love for humans without being so worried about what their color meant to everyone else around me.

In essence, I would have had the freedom to live the life that God had in store for me without having to wait thirty years to know it, feel it and step into it. **Freedom.** The word *sounds* as liberating as it *feels*. Even at the age of thirty-six I feel like I am closer to accepting the power that freedom has to offer me.

But even now, just like then, when it involves living or accepting freedom, we have a tendency to talk ourselves out of knowing what to do with freedom once we get a piece of it in our lives.

With freedom and choice come consequences. If we are ready to agree that a problem exists when it comes to the discussion of race and race relations in our society than it is fair to also say that these same problems exist on a smaller scale in our homes and in our personal relationships and networks. Some of us will allow our imaginations and ego to take over, resulting in a disconnection between who we are as racially different individuals, and who others want us to be. This was the insane confusion that I experienced for most of my life.

We must realize that there is no better stage than that of our own homes and life experiences from which to teach and educate. We can begin to engage those around us and spread a powerful message of inclusiveness and love. When we learn how to respect one another and how to communicate the very things that emanate from inside of us, we are true to our purpose and the vision we have of ourselves.

If we as parents choose to regard people based on their humanness, instead of preconceived stereotypes and prejudice, then it will be important to your child. It is important to create a foundation of openness and understanding within your family unit and the environment(s) in which your children spend most of their time. For children, especially mixed-race children, it is important to expose them to situations and individuals who account for the racial diversity that encompasses the globe.

When we surround ourselves with culturally distinct and different looking people, we give ourselves the greatest opportunity to learn and become exposed to differences and ultimately, similarities. If your child's schools or neighborhoods are homogenous, it is the parent's responsibility to find diverse groups of peers and individuals with whom your children can interact. Again, I call your attention to the idea of the frequency of these diverse contacts.

Besides the interactions and experiences with primary family members, we should be focused on expanding the interactions and experiences with friends and peers (the third layer of our racial development onion). This layer directly affects how mixed-raced children perceive themselves personally. In addition, it affects how they see themselves in relation to the images and meanings that are contextually defined by society at large.

When children look different, they are perceived differently. When children don't fit the characteristics of what it looks like and feels like to be "black" or to be "white" then we get the question, "What are you?" This question is asked by others in an attempt to clarify how they should respond to, accept and/or

170

challenge the identity offered by the different looking child.

The response of individuals, making up the social context, in relation to how biracial children self-identify has a major impact on how biracial children will ultimately come to view themselves. Social responses from individuals along with their physical appearance and the support from their families and other external factors, all play into the process of how biracial children learn to assess the degree of "whiteness" and "blackness" when expressing what's important to them. [68] Parents, caregivers, social service providers and biracial children need to know that accepting a racial self-identity can include accepting a single racial identification or many.

Authors Rockquemore and Laszloffy provide a Continuum of Biracial Identity (COBI) model that provides the option to blend an affiliation for or understanding of any one of several racial identities. [69] As individuals involved in the development and education of biracial children, it is important to note our role as responders to racial identities and educators in the options that exist for mixed-race children. "For parents and other concerned adults, it is critical to foster the development of skills that mixed-race children can use to assist them in asserting their identities in situations where they may be miscategorized or where their racial identity may be directly challenged." [70]

In order to help children cope with the miscategorization that can take part on behalf of both whites and blacks, parents can teach their children how to acknowledge the reality of their racial background that qualifies them as mixed-race individuals. They can also teach their children when and how to respond or address the challenger and they can empower their children by teaching them to become

171

comfortable defining themselves when asserting themselves. The important thing for adults and parents to understand is that there exist numerous opportunities and resources to help you in preparing your children to face the incidents of acceptance or rejection that they will face.

Making biracial children feel comfortable in their own skin will enable them to better deal with unexpected and different types of people and situations before they happen. It is good for parents to know the source of some of the internalized oppression that occurs in various relationships. Authors Rockquemore and Laszloffy point out the following motivations behind many of the relationship dynamics experienced within intraracial and interracial individuals [71]:

1. *When darker-skinned girls behave in a rejecting way toward lighter-skinned girls, this usually is motivated by their own history of feeling rejected and negatively treated because of their skin color. Unlike rejection from whites that conveys superiority, rejection from dark-skinned females is rooted in the pain of inferiority.*

2. *When white girls reject mixed-race girls, they do so from a place of privilege that communicates: "You are not white and therefore you aren't as good as I am."*

3. *When black girls reject mixed-race girls, they do so from a place of pain that screams, "You are one of those people who have hurt me and so not only are you not a part of me, but I want you to feel some of the pain I feel."*

4. *When mixed-race women honestly do think, feel, and act as if they are "better" than their darker-skinned sisters, the root cause of this sense of superiority is their internalized oppression. The flaunting of internalized superiority simultaneously projects hostility and a devaluation of blackness.*

With or without access to the parent of color, the parent and extended family members of biracial children need to realize that they can still celebrate and discuss the differences in culture, heritage and color found within the varied and colorful backgrounds of their children. Parents can learn how their biracial children develop a sense of racial identification, how that identification evolves and how it is affected by every one of their children's important relationships with family, friends and peers and the environment. Families, parents and their mixed-race children learn how mixed-race children, adolescents and young adults come to understand their racial identity in direct relation to their family members, friends, neighborhoods, schools and churches.

By "seeing" color, parents and families see their beautiful biracial child for all that they can be and should be, without giving power to the limiting stereotypes that develop when people operate out of ignorance and fear. "When parents and other adults are able to acknowledge children's blackness and whiteness, they convey a message to children that supports the acceptance and blending of their ancestry." [72]

Twenty-Three
Take the Challenge! Become a Proactive Parent

We have discussed and urged individuals raising bi-racial children to learn, understand and acknowledge race and their direct relationship with race as it pertains to their child. What we are really saying is that these same individuals need to take an immediate and proactive role in decoding and breaking down the way children's lives are bombarded and shaped by racism, sexism and ignorance. In order to do this, author and speaker bell hooks refers to parents and other adults who need to develop a "critical consciousness" which has been defined as the ability to understand and decipher the "overt and the subtle manifestations of oppressive ways of thinking, being, and doing." [73]

We assume a critical consciousness when we can look through and past what the media, in all of its forms, tries to convince us is acceptable, good and right. It is only when we begin to question what others tell us to do, how to do it and how it should affect us, that we begin to emerge from an oppressive way of life and living and move toward a freedom of self-identity, self-understanding and self-acceptance. "While it useful to broaden the definition of what is considered beautiful, it is even more helpful to support girls in seeing themselves as more than just their physical bodies. In other words, it is imperative to support girls in developing their intellectual, athletic, and spiritual capacities, which fosters the notion that they are multidimensional beings and not merely defined in terms of their bodies and beauty." [74]

Parents have a responsibility to ask their children provocative questions about messages that are being passed on through music videos, television shows or

175

"false" advertisement. Engage your children and ask them questions to determine how viewing a certain program or hearing lyrics within a song made them feel. Invite your children to begin questioning the messages that are bombarding all of us. Children will begin to see and feel a change simply from being invited to interact with adults who are bold enough to challenge their way of thinking and feeling about the world around them.

Even more important than bringing your children's attention to the goings on in the outside world will be the change that your children see within you as you engage and challenge yourself to question what we have accepted as normal and acceptable for far too long. By breaking free from oppressive mentalities, we begin to change our attitudes, thoughts and behaviors while interacting with individuals who appear and act differently than we expect them to act. If we are beginning to challenge our children we must first begin to challenge ourselves.

Begin to take notice as to whether or not you express preferential treatment to your children whose physical appearance may differ from another, depending on which parent they take after. Begin to reinforce love as the ultimate beauty standard instead of ideals that are limiting and devaluing in their very nature. Today, I challenge you to reconsider the "old" views of race and racial identification and consider the newer perspectives that seek to emphasize the social and mental perspectives associated with the journey of racial self-identification.

"New" concepts and identity models describe the various ranges of racial identifications that mixed-race children can and do develop. These "new" models are quick to point out that "no one way is better, more valuable or more correct than any other" and they challenge the "old" notions that there is only one correct way for mixed-race individuals to understand their racial identity. These new models resist attempts to "fit" mixed-race people into a singular identity. [75]

The greatest challenge for mixed-race people is adopting a racial identity that has the potential to be challenged or rejected by others in their environment. "Because mixed-race people are both white and black, but not entirely white or black, they are at risk for being targeted by both white and black people." [76] The way in which people or things within a biracial child's given environment respond, not the chosen racial identity, offers the greatest opportunity for destruction to the overall psychological health and functioning for those individuals who identify as mixed-race.

Many mixed-race people may develop several and distinct racial identities and all are valid. Mixed-race individuals are free to locate themselves anywhere within or throughout a "blending continuum" [77] that can change on a daily, weekly or monthly basis. In most cases, as is my experience, many of our racial identities change due to an experience that causes the mixed-race person to shift their previously held notions and/or ideas.

Getting people to be comfortable in order to discuss race is hard and it goes back to the idea of frequency. Even between individuals who are in a biracial relationship discussing race can become quite uncomfortable considering that most of us are operating on different racial identity levels and are using different vocabularies to express meanings and experiences. How many social settings have you been in and watched as people, family and friends, would excuse themselves from the setting rather than get caught talking about race or race relations?

For some people, there exists a fear of saying or doing the wrong thing and being accused of not knowing or having any experience from which to talk. For others, the idea of opening up and sharing a feeling or opinion, only to be shot down or rejected, is too harrowing. Ultimately, the fear of being laughed at, rejected or considered racially insensitive, prejudiced, or even racist, keeps people from talking in mono-racial and cross racial settings.

Currently in our society, two distinct extremes exist and can offer the same powerful punch. First, there is the *denial* of the obvious physical, emotional and psychological differences that exist within racial boundaries and ideologies and then there is the *acceptance* of color, traits and characteristics to a degree that isolates, undervalues and precludes emotional, psychological and racial development. These two extremes can exist within a biracial child's internal world (expressed by parents, siblings and close friends) and their external world (representing the schools, neighborhoods, churches, and independent people encountered every day in grocery and department stores). "At the same time, mixed-race children have an even more marginalized experience because they often do not 'fit' into totalizing categories of either whiteness or blackness, which places them at risk of being rejected by both groups, and of never feeling as if they truly belong anywhere." [78]

Many people today are already facing problems that can drain their energy, focus and talents. When it comes to something as sensitive and all encompassing as raising a mixed-race child, it's hard for individuals and/or families to constantly be aware and consider the issues and obstacles that are truly innate and unique to this experience. "Because of the power of race, parents raising mixed-race children have a responsibility to engage in a process of racial socialization that will prepare their children to understand and effectively negotiate the complexities of race relations." [79]

In too many cases, individuals raising biracial children feel isolated from one another, their communities and their cultures. The isolation comes from feeling like you are "doing the raising" all on your own. For the situations that exist wherein the parent of color is absent from the biracial child's life, the child and remaining parent can feel the pressure and difficulty in every situation when the child has questions or issues with living life in relation to physical appearance, certain physical traits and cultural qualities.

Pride, frustration and anger over their social or familial situations can prevent parents and families raising mixed-race children from asking for help, seeking assistance for their children or singling out a role model and/or mentor that can step in to offer advice, empowerment and cultural awareness. Issues between parents, miscommunication and divorce can all lead to families and parents missing opportunities to receive helpful information, and arm their children with positive ideas and reinforcement. Ultimately, what's missing is an opportunity to be remarkable: parent and child alike.

This book is an attempt to identify the issues that exist in households across America where families and parents find themselves raising mixed-race children. As a biracial individual I have experienced many situations and interactions that have left me questioning my heritage, ability, talents and power. Along my personal journey I tried to make sense of all the uncomfortable situations I experienced while raised in an all white household.

While trying to "find" myself and understand my purpose on this earth, it was only a matter of time

179

before I began researching the history and process of racial identity awareness. I found that there are a small group of scholars who are doing major work within this specific area and as I gathered information about this niche, I ultimately learned a lot about myself. This seems like a good place to note that this book interchangeably uses the terms "biracial", "multiracial" and "mixed-race" to describe the broadest population of individuals with mixed racial ancestry.

While my racial background is that of white/black parentage, the content and context of this book is not to be construed as specific only to the product of black/white parentage or unions. Throughout this text I have described my own mother as the perfect example of a parent who raised her biracial child with a colorblind mentality. While I know that she did the best she could with what she had, her best intentions couldn't protect me from a racially ignorant life that caused me to experience unnecessary bouts of hurt and pain. Color blind parents have to understand the power that they hold for their biracial children when it comes to whether or not their biracial child will be empowered, encouraged, devalued or destroyed.

When parents raise biracial children, all of the differences that exist need to be discussed and explained. Children need to be armed with information. While the idea of loving someone that came from you, unconditionally and without reservation, is the truest love I can imagine, there is no love in presenting an innocent child to the world to be devoured by long standing hate, prejudice, misunderstanding and injustice.

My life's journey has taken me down many paths. At some age I entered into a type of survival mode. Because I cannot pinpoint the exact age and since I can remember numerous points within my life experience, I do believe this survival mode was actually a set of several attempts to separate myself from the world.

At these specific points in my life I remember being very emotionally low. I remember being very aware of my differences and never feeling like I had the right, even if I had someone I felt I could talk with, to approach them or ask them to explain these hidden things about me. I felt hurt by the cards the world had dealt me. I felt like the butt of a cruel joke and hated looking like I did and feeling like I did without knowing why.

During my personally inflicted modes of survival I resisted every individual and situation that presented itself as an opportunity. While I ached to have a question answered the fear of these people laughing at me behind my back was enough of a deterrent in and of itself. For each moment of separation endured, a lifetime of isolation took over.

I began to pull away from friends and tried everything to avoid family situations and settings. Each time I retreated, my perfectly constructed identity placed a new brick into the wall around my heart. This process disallowed me from truly connecting with individuals who I now know had nothing but the best of intentions for me in their hearts and in their lives.

Understanding the hardness that I carried with me in my heart and in my soul I found myself concerned with the hearts and souls of other young, impressionable, biracial people who find themselves living and loving in today's world. They are without role models or mentors that can identify, empathize or understand their plight. The separation and isolation that I felt caused me to fear white people and black people.

The fear that I felt made me want to hide every-thing about myself. I was afraid of what people would say about the way I would do certain things. I had such a distorted view of myself that I believed everyone else's view or opinion of me was skewed. I didn't know how to be half white and I didn't know how to be half black.

I saw no one else doing it partly or completely. In my distorted mind I could only be fully white or fully black in order to be completely alive and accepted. In order to be comfortable and make others feel com-fortable around me, I had to be what they were. Whenever I tried to just be me, I couldn't stand the looks, the stares, the comments or the penetrating laughs behind my back.

Because of the love shown to me by my mother and the guidance and patience paid to me by my best friend and the love of my life, I engaged with God and asked that He prepare me; to instruct my purpose and make something out of this crazy, bira-cial life that I had lived and known. It was only by the grace of God that I came to understand that part of my purpose on this earth was to *Build Biracial Re-lationships and Mentor* multiracial families, mixed-race children and biracial couples. For the first time in my life, there is a meaning behind every childhood experience that made me cry.

There is value in the experiences that had for far too long, separated me from my peers and family members. I know that my life experience has some-thing to offer someone, somewhere. I believe that through any one of my experiences, feelings, admis-sions or fears, a family or parent who find themselves lucky enough to be raising children of any color now know that they have a resource, guid-ance, and a connection with someone who understands. No longer do they or I have to do anything alone.

My interactions with all of the people in my life allowed me to present and create varied opportunities to raise awareness for and of the specific issues faced by people of all colors and racial and ethnic backgrounds. I am now in a position to assist others with replacing feelings of fear and confusion with a sense of understanding and inspiration. I now focus my time and energies on empowering parents and families who I find to be very brave in their desire to raise their children, no matter their color, in a society and world that can be, at times, unforgiving.

I especially love and appreciate working with mixed race children to help them understand the options and processes available to them as they seem eager to learn and attempt to find out about all of the things that make them unique and different. I answered the call to mentorship and now find myself one of the more powerful sources of information for biracial children and every member of their family unit. Together, whether a biracial individual, a parent or family member who is raising a biracial child, or an educator impacting the life of biracial children, we can increase awareness and go forward on a foundation of love and acceptance.

Together we are strong, empowered and purposeful while helping others and ourselves understand our children's sense of self-awareness, self -identity and cultural awareness as it pertains to all aspects of this world. Together we can create dialogue within mixed-race families and biracial relationships and educate society at large about the diversity of biracial people who are living, working, learning and loving all over the world. Together we can grant truth and freedom to biracial individuals everywhere as they develop a vision for themselves within their schools, their peer circles, their families and the world.

I remember a time recently when I was asked to write down a time in my life when I wished that I had had someone that I could have talked with in order to obtain guidance and focus. I immediately thought of those instances when I wished I could have had someone in my life; someone who looked like me and understood me. I thought of those times when I needed help filling out applications, opening a bank account for the first time and dealing with people who looked at me and thought of me differently than how I looked and thought of myself.

From the time I was seven or eight, I was very aware of how different others perceived me to be from my mother. I longed for someone to guide me while communicating with my mother all of the things I wanted to ask but didn't know how. I wanted and needed someone to help me help my mother understand all of the things I wanted to say but felt too embarrassed to express. I am convinced that had I been given access to someone who understood me and looked like me, I would be a very different person today.

While working with families to identify and remove the very same obstacles I experienced as a child, I began to see and understand a common theme. Within most of the families or situations where a parent was raising a mixed-race child, the parent had given their heart entirely to the indoctrination of raising and loving their children. While doing so, they vowed to never let their precious child feel, hear or experience racism, prejudice or injustice.

It is my belief that without an open line of communication guided by trust and absent of judgment, a child will not be encouraged to go to their parent for information about differences that can, sometimes, be very obvious in their manifestations. Children have a way of absorbing information gathered from verbal and nonverbal sources. Much of what parents and families try to hide show up again.

A child can manifest a "disconnect" between perceived and real truths in many different forms. Whether the child displays violent outbursts, quiet periods of isolation or a strong resentment toward all things, the child has a way of demanding truth even when confronted with ignorance on the part of the person or people who claim to love them with no limit. "Unlike most single race children, mixed-race children have no parent with whom they can directly identify with as a mixed-race person. In other words, unless one's parent is also mixed-race, the majority of mixed-race children are learning about race from one or more adults who have not directly experienced their racial reality." [80]

What these same parents don't realize is that by wanting to protect their child from a reality of racial injustice in our nation's history and institutions, they are in fact denying the existence of racial differences that exist between their skin color and the color of their child. The meaning of denying a legacy and a history is the same as denying an understanding, awareness and an identity. This act could lead to confusion and hatred within their child that is so deeply rooted that the effects could last for generations to come.

Parents need to prepare themselves to be the source of cultural, historical and relational information for their biracial child, especially in situations where the biracial child is not living with or connected to the parent of color. "Moreover, the more actively parents racially socialize their children, the more likely children are to develop a stronger sense

185

of self-esteem, have higher rates of academic achievement and lower rates of disciplinary problems, and appear to be more psychologically well adjusted overall." [81]

I think we can all agree that the world is confusing and unfair on its own. Every parent raising a child that looks different from their mother or father should be encouraged to ask questions and find people who can serve as positive influences and role models in their child's life. While some experiences and traits can be shared between parent and child, parents must recognize and value the differences that are sure to exist.

More importantly, parents must understand and communicate to everyone that they understand the uniqueness of their situation. Know that it is ok to say, "I am raising a biracial child". Now feel it and accept it. By saying this, you signify that, as parents, you understand how significant your child's life experience is going to be. Rise to the occasion to provide the most and best resources, knowledge and input. Insert an open line of communication into your daily life and communicate a sense of love and understanding. Let everything about your being and doing be guided by trust, not judgment.

Parents should be the first source of all good, relevant and applicable information their child receives on race, cultural awareness and identity. If a parent allows the bad, negative or uncomfortable aspects of their own life experience to be the basis for which they interact with their biracial children than that parent is setting their child up for failure of a monumental sort. Whether parents consciously or unconsciously withhold truth and facts from their child or fail to explain the legacy and history of race and race relations, the child is more prone to experience issues with embarrassment, prejudices, behavioral issues, anger and sadly, self-hatred. "Parents need to convey that they see how their child-children's mixed-race status provides the benefit of being able to relate to both whiteness and blackness, and the challenges of never feeling completely a part of either world." [82]

In situations where biracial parents are experiencing the effects of a divorce, children are unable to separate the role race plays within the demise of the relationship. Children in the household will usually side with the parent who continues to provide emotional, monetary and physical support and will most likely pick up on any racial undertones, overtly or covertly expressed by the custodial parent. Unfortunately, children also have the ability to internalize a lot of what they see, hear and feel and will begin to shift the blame for the absent parents onto themselves. Any type of hatred or loathing expressed in verbalized racial undertones toward one parent or another will be taken by the biracial child as an attack on that part of them that makes up or identifies with the race that is being disparaged.

Twenty-Four
What Have We Learned?

So let's ask ourselves what have we learned? We know that extremes exist in this world when it comes to the way people deal with the manifestation of race. There are also limits.

Limits exist in the sense of what children can take in and deal with on a daily basis or within the context of their adolescent or teenage life. I believe that many of the issues that I brought into adulthood were carried with me on a blank slate. And this is the problem.

While others were able to arm themselves during their transition from childhood into teenage years with information, feelings and situations experienced by one or both of their parents, I was left alone with no preparation or outlet to absorb the shock of racism and prejudice. Glaringly missing from my life was a reason for my skin color being different than that of my mother and my sister. I had no one who was able to or willing to provide me with an explanation for the thickness of my thighs or the tightness of the curls in my hair as compared to my white mother and sister.

It is my goal to educate mixed-race families and biracial individuals of the options that exist outside of the limited categorization choices that currently exist in our society. With the onset of cutting edge research, the changes in the US Census forms and new approaches to learning about the mixed-race experience, biracial individuals have been given a new way to define race and racial identity as it pertains to their life experience and the things that affect them on a daily or moment-by-moment basis. Gone are the days that your appearance and physical traits force you to have to act a certain way or identify exclusively with a certain group of individuals based solely on race.

Identity is redefined as "the way we understand ourselves in relation to others and our social environment." Identity should be seen as a "social process" and constantly evolving and responding to others and the environments in which we find our children in schools, friend circles, neighborhoods and families. It is my goal as a biracial human being to seek to explore how educational systems; community programs, biracial children, mixed-race families and biracial couples receive, interpret and manifest how others relate to them.

Healthy relationships within any one of these social dynamics should include an open door communication policy that integrates honesty and openness about how every day life is directly related to and shaped by race and its subsequent legacy in prejudice and stereotyping. Without first knowing where you stand as a mono-racial individual raising mixed-race children or involved in a biracial relationship it is highly unlikely that you will develop a higher sense of understanding and knowledge of your own racial identity development. The same can be said for biracial individuals or any person of color raising children or involved in a biracial relationship.

Without ever having to defend one's racial representation, or without an opportunity to share details of a life experience or situation, people are left without significant inroads to communicate ideas, attitudes and opinions about challenges, negotiations or inappropriate conditions. One of the ideas communicated in my daily blog and interaction with people is that children today don't have to grow up with or silently endure the issues that I and other biracial individuals have experienced. Parents can educate themselves on how to communicate with their children about the ideological, institutional and individual types of racism that exist in our society today.

By creating this type of open dialogue, parents take a proactive approach in helping their children feel a sense of "self love" and understand the many options that exist to tap into a multitude of available racial self-identifications. Parents become a part of the process their biracial children engage in when learning how to deal and cope with environmental factors and people that will test their children's racial boundaries and ideas of racial justice.

You don't have to do it alone. Resources exist and people care. I care. If anything about the experiences outlined in this book speak to you or your experience, as a parent or a child, please reach out and ask for help. Ask for guidance in focusing your energy on increasing your ability to communicate effectively, lovingly and with respect. Find an interactive lifeline that fits your style and needs and let it help you conquer and surpass your greatest fears.

Dr. Dyer defines fear as 'false evidence appearing real'. [83] In too many of our lives, we approach one another in fear and all things that come from this interaction can affect one another, our families and our communities. We should be confident in our approach with each other and interact with one another after removing fear from our experiences.

When you erase fear, you are dealing in truth. Truth reveals an honesty that surpasses hate, resentment and insecurities.

> *"As bell hooks states: 'Only love can give us the strength to go forward in the midst of heartbreak and misery. Only love can give us the power to reconcile, to redeem, the power to renew our weary spirits and save lost souls.*

The transformative power of love is the foundation of all meaningful social change. Without love our lives are without meaning.'[84]
James McBride echoes this sentiment in his book entitled, The Color of Water: A Black Man's Tribute to his White Mother. In James' book, I learned the importance of telling my story. Just like James said [85]:

"One of the nicer things that has happened as a result of the book's publication is that people of mixed race have found a bit of their own story in these pages. I have met hundreds of mixed-race people of all types, and I'm happy to report that-guess what, folks- they're happy, normal people! They're finding a way. Grandparents and grandchildren, husbands and wives, cousins and second cousins. And they will continue to strive and thrive. The plain truth is that you'd have an easier time standing in the middle of the Mississippi River and requesting that it flow backward then to expect people of different races and backgrounds to stop loving each other, stop marrying each other, stop starting families, stop enjoying dreams that love inspires. Love is unstoppable. It is our greatest weapon, a natural force, created by God."

James, your words were insightful and your story: truly an inspiration. Thank you!

And thank you to my mother. While your sources for help and understanding were limited, you could have easily given me up and given up a chance to love me. You didn't. In the face of family sneers and ungodly friends, you chose to keep me and love me with all that you had and all that you were.

Because of your sheer, unadulterated love, I have learned what it is to love and be loved. While we have had our issues and differences along the way, I always knew that they were second place to the love that we expressed for one another. Mother, I thank you for being open to learning about me and for accepting me as I journeyed through the first half of my biracial life.

I thank God for you every single day because I know that any other alternative would not have allowed me to experience a relationship such as the one we share. I love you and am proud of you. I hope you learn to celebrate your experience just as I have learned to celebrate mine.

And in gratitude to my late my father: in the brief time that we had together here on earth, I thank you for welcoming me into your life and heart with open arms. Thank you for allowing me to experience what I always imagined it would feel like to be protected, wanted and paraded around by a loving father. You had so much to teach and I, so much to learn.

I thank you for the phone calls when you would ask me how I was doing. I thank you for the times you would call because you wanted me to know that you were thinking of me. Thank you for your honesty and for setting things straight and for not caring about keeping up appearances. When I called, you came. When I asked, you answered. For these things, I love you and I thank you.

I am especially grateful to my dearest Philip. I remember standing with you on the PATH train platform at Exchange Place in Jersey City. We were waiting for the train that would take us into NYC. I remember standing there with you and thinking to myself that I was so lucky to have you in my life. Little did I know that your encouragement would lead me to ask my mother about my father which in turn led me straight to finding him, being loved by him and coming to peace with all that I have and all that I am.

No one else has ever had such an impact on my life. I thank God for you every single day and I owe the condition of my heart to you. You ignited within me the hope and inspiration which began a process of healing that has led me to be able to come to terms with all that I am and all that I have to offer to other people who look and feel just like me. You will always be the key to my puzzle of life and I thank you for being you.

Don't ever change.

APPENDIX

2010 US Census Data

[As written in the 2010 US Census Briefing] [37]
http://www.census.gov/prod/cen2010/briefs/c2
010br-02.pdf:

Race

The OMB definitions of the race categories used in the 2010 Census, plus the Census Bureau's definition of Some Other Race, are presented in the text box "Definition of Race Categories Used in the 2010 Census." Starting in 1997, OMB required federal agencies to use a minimum of five race categories: White, Black or African American, American Indian or Alaska Native, Asian, and Native Hawaiian or Other Pacific Islander. For respondents unable to identify with any of these five race categories, OMB approved the Census Bureau's inclusion of a sixth category—Some Other Race—on the Census 2000 and 2010 Census questionnaires.

Data on race have been collected since the first U.S. decennial census in 1790. For the first time in Census 2000, individuals were presented with the option to self-identify with more than one race and this continued with the 2010 Census, as prescribed by OMB. There are 57 possible multiple race combinations involving the five OMB race categories and Some Other Race.

The 2010 Census question on race included 15 separate response categories and three areas where respondents could write-in detailed information about their race. The response categories and write-in answers can be combined to create the five minimum OMB race categories plus Some Other Race. In addition to White, Black or African American, American Indian and Alaska Native, and Some Other Race, 7 of the 15 response categories are Asian groups and 4 are Native Hawaiian and Other Pacific Islander groups. [*There were two changes to the question on race for the 2010 Census. First, the wording of the race question was changed from "What is this person's race? Mark one or more races to indicate what this person considers himself/herself to be" in 2000 to "What is this person's race? Mark one or more boxes" for 2010. Second, in 2010, examples were added to the "Other Asian" response category (Hmong, Laotian, Thai, Pakistani, Cambodian, and so on) and the "Other Pacific Islander" response category (Fijian, Tongan, and so on). In 2000, no examples were given in the race question.*

The race categories included in the census questionnaire generally reflect a social definition of race recognized in this country and are not an attempt to define race biologically, anthropologically, or genetically. In addition, it is recognized that the categories of the race question include race and national origin or sociocultural group]

Definition of Race Categories Used in the 2010 Census

- "White" refers to a person having origins in any of the original peoples of Europe, the Middle East, or North Africa. It includes people who indicated their race(s) as "White" or reported entries such as Irish, German, Italian, Lebanese, Arab, Moroccan, or Caucasian.

- "Black or African American" refers to a person having origins in any of the Black racial groups of Africa. It includes people who indicated their race(s) as "Black, African Am., or

Negro" or reported entries such as African American, Kenyan, Nigerian, or Haitian.

- "American Indian or Alaska Native" refers to a person having origins in any of the original peoples of North and South America (including Central America) and who maintains tribal affiliation or community attachment. This category includes people who indicated their race(s) as "American Indian or Alaska Native" or reported their enrolled or principal tribe, such as Navajo, Blackfeet, Inupiat, Yup'ik, or Central American Indian groups or South American Indian groups.

- "Asian" refers to a person having origins in any of the original peoples of the Far East, Southeast Asia, or the Indian subcontinent, including, for example, Cambodia, China, India, Japan, Korea, Malaysia, Pakistan, the Philippine Islands, Thailand, and Vietnam. It includes people who indicated their race(s) as "Asian" or reported entries such as "Asian Indian," "Chinese," "Filipino," "Korean," "Japanese," "Vietnamese," and "Other Asian" or provided other detailed Asian responses.

- "Native Hawaiian or Other Pacific Islander" refers to a person having origins in any of the original peoples of Hawaii, Guam, Samoa, or other Pacific Islands. It includes people who indicated their race(s) as "Pacific Islander" or reported entries such as "Native Hawaiian," "Guamanian or Chamorro," "Samoan," and "Other Pacific Islander" or provided other detailed Pacific Islander responses.

- "Some Other Race" includes all other responses not included in the White, Black or African American, American Indian or Alaska Native, Asian, and Native Hawaiian or Other Pacific Islander race categories described above. Respondents reporting entries such as multiracial, mixed, interracial, or a Hispanic or Latino group (for example, Mexican, Puerto Rican, Cuban, or Spanish) in response to the race question are included in this category.

RACE AND HISPANIC ORIGIN IN THE 2010 CENSUS

Data from the 2010 Census provide insights to our racially and ethnically diverse nation. According to the 2010 Census, 308.7 million people resided in the United States on April 1, 2010—an increase of 27.3 million people, or 9.7 percent, between 2000 and 2010. The vast majority of the growth in the total population came from increases in those who reported their race(s) as something other than White alone and those who reported their ethnicity as Hispanic or Latino.

More than half of the growth in the total population of the United States between 2000 and 2010 was due to the increase in the Hispanic population.

In 2010, there were 50.5 million Hispanics in the United States, composing 16 percent of the total population. Between 2000 and 2010, the Hispanic population grew by 43 percent—rising from 35.3 million in 2000, when this group made up 13 percent of the total population. The Hispanic population increased by 15.2 million between 2000 and 2010, accounting for over half of the 27.3 million increase in the total population of the United States.

The non-Hispanic population grew relatively slower over the decade, about 5 percent. Within the non-

Hispanic population, the number of people who reported their race as White alone grew even slower be-between 2000 and 2010 (1 percent). While the non-Hispanic White alone population increased numerically from 194.6 million to 196.8 million over the 10-year period, its proportion of the total population declined from 69 percent to 64 percent. [*For the purposes of this report, the term "reported" is used to refer to the response provided by respondents as well as responses assigned during the editing and imputation process. The observed changes in race and Hispanic origin counts between Census 2000 and the 2010 Census could be attributed to a number of factors. Demographic change since 2000, which includes births and deaths in a geographic area and migration in and out of a geographic area, will have an impact on the resulting 2010 Census counts. Additionally, some changes in the race and Hispanic origin questions' wording and format since Census 2000 could have influenced reporting patterns in the 2010 Census.*]

The overwhelming majority of the total population of the United States reported only one race in 2010.

In the 2010 Census, 97 percent of all respondents (299.7 million) reported only one race. The largest group reported White alone (223.6 million), accounting for 72 percent of all people living in the United States. The Black or African-American alone population was 38.9 million and represented 13 percent of the total population. There were 2.9 million respondents who indicated American Indian and Alaska Native alone (0.9 percent). Approximately 14.7 million (about 5 percent of all respondents) identified their race as Asian alone. The smallest major race group was Native Hawaiian and Other Pacific Islander alone (0.5 million) and represented 0.2 percent of the total population. The remainder of respondents who reported only one race—19.1 million (6 percent of all respondents) - were classified as Some Other Race alone. People who reported more than one race numbered 9.0 million in the 2010 Census and made up about 3 percent of the total population. *[Individuals who responded to the question on race by indicating only one race are referred to as the race-alone population or the group that reported only one race category. Six categories make up this population: White alone, Black or African American alone, American Indian and Alaska Native alone, Asian alone, Native Hawaiian and Other Pacific Islander alone, and Some Other Race alone. Individuals who chose more than 1 of the 6 race categories are referred to as the Two or More Races population. All respondents who indicated more than one race can be collapsed into the Two or More Races category which, combined with the six race-alone categories, yields seven mutually exclusive and exhaustive categories. Thus, the six race-alone categories and the Two or More Races category sum to the total population. As a matter of policy, the Census Bureau does not advocate the use of the alone population over the alone-or-in-combination population or vice versa. The use of the alone population in sections of this report does not imply that it is a preferred method of presenting or analyzing data. The same is true for sections of this report that focus on the alone-or-in-combination population. Data on race from the 2010 Census can be presented and discussed in a variety of ways. The terms "Black or African American" and "Black" are used interchangeably in this report.]*

The Asian population grew faster than any other major race group between 2000 and 2010.

In the United States, all major race groups increased in population size between 2000 and 2010, but they grew at different rates. Over the decade, the Asian alone population experienced the fastest rate of growth and the White alone population experienced the slowest rate of growth, with the other major race groups' growth spanning the range in between. Of the 27.3 million people added to the total population of the United States between 2000 and 2010, the White alone population made up just under half of the growth—increasing 12.1 million. Within the White alone population, the vast majority of the growth was propelled by the Hispanic population.

The Asian alone population increased by 43 percent between 2000 and 2010, more than any other major race group. The Asian alone population had the second-largest numeric change (4.4 million), growing from 10.2 million in 2000 to 14.7 million in 2010. The Asian alone population gained the most in share of the total population, moving up from about 4 percent in 2000 to about 5 percent in 2010.

The Native Hawaiian and Other Pacific Islander alone population, the smallest major race group, also grew substantially between 2000 and 2010, increasing by more than one-third. This population numbered 398,835 in 2000, rising to 540,013 in 2010 with its proportion of the total population changing from 0.1 percent to 0.2 percent, respectively.

Between 2000 and 2010, the population classified as Some Other Race alone increased considerably, growing by about one-quarter. This population climbed from 15.4 million in 2000 to 19.1 million in 2010 and was approximately 6 percent of the total population in both decennial censuses. Most of this growth was due to increases in the Hispanic population.

An 18 percent growth in the American Indian and Alaska Native alone population occurred between 2000 and 2010. This population, also relatively small numerically, maintained its proportion of the total population between decennial censuses (0.9 percent) while growing from 2.5 million to 2.9 million.

While the Black alone population had the third-largest numeric increase in population size over the decade (4.3 million), behind the White alone and Asian alone populations, it grew slower than most other major race groups. In fact, the Black alone population exhibited the smallest percentage growth outside of the White alone population, increasing 12 percent between 2000 and 2010. This population rose from 34.7 million in 2000 to 38.9 million in 2010, making up 12 percent and 13 percent of the total population, respectively.

The only major race group to experience a decrease in its proportion of the total population was the White alone population. While this group increased the most numerically between decennial censuses (211.5 million to 223.6 million), its share of the total population fell from 75 percent in 2000 to 72 percent in 2010.

The Two or More Races population was one of the fastest-growing groups over the decade. This population increased approximately one-third between 2000 and 2010.

It should be known that the US Census 2010 makes the following notation:

In Census 2000, an error in data processing resulted in an overstatement of the Two or More Races population by about 1 million people (about 15 percent) nationally, which almost entirely affected race combinations involving Some Other Race. Therefore, data users should assess observed changes in the Two or More Races population and race combinations involving Some Other Race between Census 2000 and the 2010 Census with caution. Changes in specific multiple-race combinations not involving Some Other Race, such as White **and** Black or White **and** Asian, generally, should be more comparable.

NOTES

1. Eduardo Bonilla-Silva. "Racism Without Racists: Color-Blind Racism and the Persistence of Racial Inequality in the United States." Rowman & Littlefield Publishers, Inc. 2003
2. Kerry Ann Rockquemore and Tracey Laszloffy. "Raising Biracial Children." Oxford, UK: AltaMira Press 2005
3. Kerry Ann Rockquemore and Tracey Laszloffy. "Raising Biracial Children." Oxford, UK: AltaMira Press 2005
4. Kerry Ann Rockquemore and Tracey Laszloffy. "Raising Biracial Children." Oxford, UK: AltaMira Press 2005
5. Kerry Ann Rockquemore and Tracey Laszloffy. "Raising Biracial Children." Oxford, UK: AltaMira Press 2005
6. Albert Memmi b. 1920, Tunis), French-language Tunisian novelist and author of numerous sociological studies treating the subject of human oppression.
7. Eduardo Bonilla-Silva. "Racism Without Racists: Color-Blind Racism and the Persistence of Racial Inequality in the United States." Rowman & Littlefield Publishers, Inc. 2003
8. Kerry Ann Rockquemore and Tracey Laszloffy. "Raising Biracial Children." Oxford, UK: AltaMira Press 2005
9. Kerry Ann Rockquemore and Tracey Laszloffy. "Raising Biracial Children." Oxford, UK: AltaMira Press 2005
10. Kerry Ann Rockquemore and Tracey Laszloffy. "Raising Biracial Children." Oxford, UK: AltaMira Press 2005

11.   Kerry Ann Rockquemore and Tracey Laszloffy. "Raising Biracial Children." Oxford, UK: AltaMira Press 2005

12.   Kerry Ann Rockquemore and Tracey Laszloffy. "Raising Biracial Children." Oxford, UK: AltaMira Press 2005

13.   Eduardo Bonilla-Silva. "Racism Without Racists: Color-Blind Racism and the Persistence of Racial Inequality in the United States." Rowman & Littlefield Publishers, Inc. 2003

14.   Kerry Ann Rockquemore and Tracey Laszloffy. "Raising Biracial Children." Oxford, UK: AltaMira Press 2005

15.   Kerry Ann Rockquemore and Tracey Laszloffy. "Raising Biracial Children." Oxford, UK: AltaMira Press 2005

16.   Kerry Ann Rockquemore and Tracey Laszloffy. "Raising Biracial Children." Oxford, UK: AltaMira Press 2005

17.   Kerry Ann Rockquemore and Tracey Laszloffy. "Raising Biracial Children." Oxford, UK: AltaMira Press 2005

18.   Kerry Ann Rockquemore and Tracey Laszloffy. "Raising Biracial Children." Oxford, UK: AltaMira Press 2005

19.   Eduardo Bonilla-Silva. "Racism Without Racists: Color-Blind Racism and the Persistence of Racial Inequality in the United States." Rowman & Littlefield Publishers, Inc. 2003

20.   Eduardo Bonilla-Silva. "Racism Without Racists: Color-Blind Racism and the Persistence of Racial Inequality in the United States." Rowman & Littlefield Publishers, Inc. 2003

21.	Eduardo Bonilla-Silva. "Racism Without Racists: Color-Blind Racism and the Persistence of Racial Inequality in the United States." Rowman & Littlefield Publishers, Inc. 2003

22.	Eduardo Bonilla-Silva. "Racism Without Racists: Color-Blind Racism and the Persistence of Racial Inequality in the United States." Rowman & Littlefield Publishers, Inc. 2003

23.	Kerry Ann Rockquemore and Tracey Laszloffy. "Raising Biracial Children." Oxford, UK: AltaMira Press 2005

24.	Kerry Ann Rockquemore and Tracey Laszloffy. "Raising Biracial Children." Oxford, UK: AltaMira Press 2005

25.	Tukufu Zuberi. "Thicker than Blood: How Racial Statistics Lie." The Regents of the University of Minnesota 2001

26.	Tukufu Zuberi. "Thicker than Blood: How Racial Statistics Lie." The Regents of the University of Minnesota 2001

27.	Eduardo Bonilla-Silva. "Racism Without Racists: Color-Blind Racism and the Persistence of Racial Inequality in the United States." Rowman & Littlefield Publishers, Inc. 2003

28.	Tukufu Zuberi. "Thicker than Blood: How Racial Statistics Lie." The Regents of the University of Minnesota 2001

29.	Tukufu Zuberi. "Thicker than Blood: How Racial Statistics Lie." The Regents of the University of Minnesota 2001

30.	Tukufu Zuberi. "Thicker than Blood: How Racial Statistics Lie." The Regents of the University of Minnesota 2001

31. Tukufu Zuberi. "Thicker than Blood: How Racial Statistics Lie." The Regents of the University of Minnesota 2001

32. Tukufu Zuberi. "Thicker than Blood: How Racial Statistics Lie." The Regents of the University of Minnesota 2001

33. Tukufu Zuberi. "Thicker than Blood: How Racial Statistics Lie." The Regents of the University of Minnesota 2001

34. Tukufu Zuberi. "Thicker than Blood: How Racial Statistics Lie." The Regents of the University of Minnesota 2001

35. Kerry Ann Rockquemore and Tracey Laszloffy. "Raising Biracial Children." Oxford, UK: AltaMira Press 2005

36. Kerry Ann Rockquemore and Tracey Laszloffy. "Raising Biracial Children." Oxford, UK: AltaMira Press 2005

37. Maya Rock '02. "What are you?" For multiracial students, declaring an identity can be complicated. Princeton Alumni Weekly January 13, 2010.

38. 2010 US Census Brief

39. http://www.census.gov/prod/cen2010/briefs/c2010br-02.pdf

40. Francis C. Assisi (2005). "Indian-American Scholar Susan Koshy Probes Interracial Sex"

41. Russell, Wilson, and Hall. "The Color Complex: The Politics of Skin Color among African Americans." First Anchor Books 1992

42. Russell, Wilson, and Hall. "The Color Complex: The Politics of Skin Color among African Americans." First Anchor Books 1992

43. United States Declaration of Independence- The quotation "All men are created equal" is arguably the best-known phrase in

any political document of the United States of America. Thomas Jefferson first used the phrase in the Declaration of Independence as a rebuttal to the going political theory of the day: the Divine Right of Kings. It was thereafter quoted or incorporated into speeches by a wide array of substantial figures in American political and social life in the United States. Thomas Day (22 June 1748 – 28 September 1789) was a British author and abolitionist. He was well-known for the children's book The History of Sandford and Merton (1783-1789) which emphasized Rousseauvian educational ideals. Jefferson borrowed the expression from an Italian friend and neighbor, Philip Mazzei, as noted by Joint Resolution 175 of the 103rd Congress as well as by John F. Kennedy in "A Nation Of Immigrants."

44.   Armitage, David. The Declaration Of Independence: A Global History. 76–77. Cambridge, Massachusetts: Harvard University Press, 2007
45.   The Gettysburg Address, Abraham Lincoln's most famous speech and one of the most quoted political speeches in United States history, was delivered at the dedication of the Soldiers' National Cemetery in Gettysburg, Pennsylvania on November 19, 1863, during the American Civil War, four and a half months after the Battle of Gettysburg. There are several sources of the speech; five known manuscript copies of the Gettysburg Address are each named for the associated person who received it from Lincoln. All versions differ in their wording, punctuation, and structure. Excerpted from Gettysburg Address on Wikipedia, The Free Encyclopedia.

46.   Historynow.org. Judith Wellman. The Seneca Falls Convention: Setting the National Stage for Women's Suffrage, Retrieved April 27, 2009- Elizabeth Cady Stanton and Lucretia Mott, two American activists in the movement to abolish slavery called together the first conference to address Women's rights and issues in Seneca Falls, New York, in 1848. Part of the reason for doing so had been that Mott had been refused permission to speak at the world anti-slavery convention in London, even though she had been an official delegate. Applying the analysis of human freedom developed in the Abolitionist movement, Stanton and others began the public career of modern feminist analysis. The Declaration of the Seneca Falls Convention, using the model of the US Declaration of Independence, forthrightly demanded that the rights of women as right-bearing individuals be acknowledged and respected by society. It was signed by sixty-eight women and thirty-two men.

47.   "I Have a Dream" Speech- **The Fulfillment of America-** On August 28, 1963, nearly one hundred years after Lincoln's Gettysburg Address, Dr. Martin Luther King, Jr., delivered the keynote address at the "March on Washington for Jobs and Freedom." Speaking on the steps of the Lincoln Memorial to a crowd of over a quarter million, King reminded the nation of the gap that separated America's promise from its fulfillment. He spoke of a dream "deeply rooted in the American dream, that one day this nation will rise up and live out the true meaning of its creed—'we hold these truths to be self-evident, that all men are created equal.'" For this dream to become a re-

ality, America would have to become a nation where individuals would "not be judged by the color of their skin but by the content of their character." King's speech played a pivotal role in persuading Congress to pass the Civil Rights Act of 1964 and Voting Rights Act of 1965, landmark legislation that finally put teeth into the constitutional bite of the 13th, 14th, and 15th Amendments. The challenge of American self-government, to secure the equal rights of all through the consent of the governed, remains not only the great task of every generation of Americans, but also that of every free society that chooses to secure the blessings of liberty for themselves and their posterity. [Wikipedia]

48.   Eduardo Bonilla-Silva. "Racism Without Racists: Color-Blind Racism and the Persistence of Racial Inequality in the United States." Rowman & Littlefield Publishers, Inc. 2003

49.   Eduardo Bonilla-Silva. "Racism Without Racists: Color-Blind Racism and the Persistence of Racial Inequality in the United States." Rowman & Littlefield Publishers, Inc. 2003

50.   Loretta I. Winters and Herman L. DeBose. "New Faces in a Changing America." Sage Publications, Inc. 2003

51.   Loretta I. Winters and Herman L. DeBose. "New Faces in a Changing America." Sage Publications, Inc. 2003

52.   Kerry Ann Rockquemore and Tracey Laszloffy. "Raising Biracial Children." Oxford, UK: AltaMira Press 2005

53. Russell, Wilson, and Hall. "The Color Complex: The Politics of Skin Color among African Americans." First Anchor Books 1992

54. Russell, Wilson, and Hall. "The Color Complex: The Politics of Skin Color among African Americans." First Anchor Books 1992

55. Russell, Wilson, and Hall. "The Color Complex: The Politics of Skin Color among African Americans." First Anchor Books 1992

56. Russell, Wilson, and Hall. "The Color Complex: The Politics of Skin Color among African Americans." First Anchor Books 1992

57. Russell, Wilson, and Hall. "The Color Complex: The Politics of Skin Color among African Americans." First Anchor Books 1992

58. Russell, Wilson, and Hall. "The Color Complex: The Politics of Skin Color among African Americans." First Anchor Books 1992

59. Tukufu Zuberi. "Thicker than Blood: How Racial Statistics Lie." The Regents of the University of Minnesota 2001

60. Kerry Ann Rockquemore and Tracey Laszloffy. "Raising Biracial Children." Oxford, UK: AltaMira Press 2005

61. Kerry Ann Rockquemore and Tracey Laszloffy. "Raising Biracial Children." Oxford, UK: AltaMira Press 2005

62. Kerry Ann Rockquemore and Tracey Laszloffy. "Raising Biracial Children." Oxford, UK: AltaMira Press 2005

63. Russell, Wilson, and Hall. "The Color Complex: The Politics of Skin Color among African Americans." First Anchor Books 1992

64. James McBride. "The Color of Water: A Black Man's Tribute to His White Mother." Berkley Publishing Group 1996

65.   Kerry Ann Rockquemore and Tracey Laszloffy. "Raising Biracial Children." Oxford, UK: AltaMira Press 2005

66.   Kerry Ann Rockquemore and Tracey Laszloffy. "Raising Biracial Children." Oxford, UK: AltaMira Press 2005

67.   Kerry Ann Rockquemore and Tracey Laszloffy. "Raising Biracial Children." Oxford, UK: AltaMira Press 2005

68.   Kerry Ann Rockquemore and Tracey Laszloffy. "Raising Biracial Children." Oxford, UK: AltaMira Press 2005

69.   Kerry Ann Rockquemore and Tracey Laszloffy. "Raising Biracial Children." Oxford, UK: AltaMira Press 2005

70.   Kerry Ann Rockquemore and Tracey Laszloffy. "Raising Biracial Children." Oxford, UK: AltaMira Press 2005

71.   Kerry Ann Rockquemore and Tracey Laszloffy. "Raising Biracial Children." Oxford, UK: AltaMira Press 2005

72.   Kerry Ann Rockquemore and Tracey Laszloffy. "Raising Biracial Children." Oxford, UK: AltaMira Press 2005

73.   Kerry Ann Rockquemore and Tracey Laszloffy. "Raising Biracial Children." Oxford, UK: AltaMira Press 2005

74.   Kerry Ann Rockquemore and Tracey Laszloffy. "Raising Biracial Children." Oxford, UK: AltaMira Press 2005

75.   Kerry Ann Rockquemore and Tracey Laszloffy. "Raising Biracial Children." Oxford, UK: AltaMira Press 2005

76.   Kerry Ann Rockquemore and Tracey Laszloffy. "Raising Biracial Children." Oxford, UK: AltaMira Press 2005

77.   Kerry Ann Rockquemore and Tracey Laszloffy. "Raising Biracial Children." Oxford, UK: AltaMira Press 2005

78.   Kerry Ann Rockquemore and Tracey Laszloffy. "Raising Biracial Children." Oxford, UK: AltaMira Press 2005

79.   Kerry Ann Rockquemore and Tracey Laszloffy. "Raising Biracial Children." Oxford, UK: AltaMira Press 2005

80.   Kerry Ann Rockquemore and Tracey Laszloffy. "Raising Biracial Children." Oxford, UK: AltaMira Press 2005

81.   Kerry Ann Rockquemore and Tracey Laszloffy. "Raising Biracial Children." Oxford, UK: AltaMira Press 2005

82.   Kerry Ann Rockquemore and Tracey Laszloffy. "Raising Biracial Children." Oxford, UK: AltaMira Press 2005

83.   Inspiration by Dr. Wayne W. Dyer pg. 169 "...the word fear is just an acronym for False Evidence Appearing Real."

84.   Kerry Ann Rockquemore and Tracey Laszloffy. "Raising Biracial Children." Oxford, UK: AltaMira Press 2005

85.   James McBride. "The Color of Water: A Black Man's Tribute to His White Mother." Berkley Publishing Group 1996

REFERENCES

1. Kerry Ann Rockquemore and Tracey Laszloffy. "Raising Biracial Children." Oxford, UK: Alta-Mira Press 2005

2. Russell, Wilson, and Hall. "The Color Complex: The Politics of Skin Color among African Americans." First Anchor Books 1992

3. Tukufu Zuberi. "Thicker than Blood: How Racial Statistics Lie." The Regents of the University of Minnesota 2001

4. James McBride. "The Color of Water: A Black Man's Tribute to His White Mother." Berkley Publishing Group 1996

5. Eduardo Bonilla-Silva. "Racism Without Racists: Color-Blind Racism and the Persistence of Racial Inequality in the United States." Rowman & Littlefield Publishers, Inc. 2003

6. Loretta I. Winters and Herman L. DeBose. "New Faces in a Changing America." Sage Publications, Inc. 2003

7. Maya Rock '02. "What are you?" Princeton Alumni Weekly January 13, 2010

CPSIA information can be obtained at www.ICGtesting.com
Printed in the USA
LVOW051048140313

324288LV00007B/55/P